PHOTOGRAPHIC MEMORIES

A Story of Shinjitsu

Risa Shimoda and Bob Fleshner

R&B Press

"Midori Shimoda represents one of the many individual tragedies of the war." -- *J. Gordon Hargrove, hearing officer, Federal Bureau of Investigation, September 24, 1942*

"For your information, I have received a copy of another order
dated May 4, 1943, directing that Midori Arthur Shimoda be
interned." --*John Edgar Hoover, Director, FBI, May 21, 1943. Sent
via confidential messenger to Colonel L. R. Forney, Assistant Chief of
Staff War Department*

"I concluded that a young man as bright as this alien was and
is thoroughly equipped, might be dangerous running loose." --
Dan Shields, US Attorney, Utah, September 1, 1943

SHINJITSU: *truth, reality*

PART ONE

CHAPTER ONE

Monte Carlo, Monaco

July 4, 1975

Adjusting the straps of her dusty backpack, Risa confidently strode up to the impossibly determined- looking, uniformed sentry who stood at attention at the entrance to the palace.

"Hi," she began, "I'm here to see Princess Grace."

As the sentry stopped to engage Risa, she noticed just how large his helmet was. She leaned back as the soldier seemingly from another era changed his forward-fixed gaze as if wanting her to repeat the question. Risa's traveling companions drew close to join her in discussion with the sentry in front of the imposing fortress. Betraying little emotion, and speaking unaccented English, the sentry inquired, "whom shall I tell Princess Grace is here to see her?"

"Risa Shimoda. I'm Midori Shimoda's daughter."

The sentry disappeared through the tall stone archway and entered the palace.

Risa stared at the ornate stonework above the entryway, and then let her eyes wander over the windows that surrounded the archway, each encased in beige stone carvings. She fumbled in the pocket of her cargo shorts until she found the small rock with the worn indentation. She rubbed it several times and smiled.

"You can't think that we're going to get in there," her friend Bill intoned as he gestured toward the castle, his flannel shirt flapping in the breeze that caught and gently moved, his thick hair as well.

"We're about to find out," Risa replied as she turned toward the sentry who was emerging from the castle and striding purposefully towards them. She held tightly to the rock called "Thumbprint" as she faced the man whose uniform matched his countenance.

"Princess Grace has asked that I see you in," the sentry informed the small group in a voice way too solemn for the occasion.

CHAPTER TWO

Kumamoto, Japan

April 1917

Midori held his grandmother's gaze as she approached, her arthritic right hand clutching a small clump of incense. His tiny body hugged the chair as though it were held in place by adhesive.

"You are seven years old, Midori," Grandma Shimoda intoned. "You are a Shimoda. A Samurai's grandson. You must learn to act like the person you are meant to be," Grandma continued as she held the little boy's gaze. "When little boys do not act the right way we must take steps to guide them."

Grandma's gait was steady, though not intimidating. She slipped past Midori, who tried in vain to keep her in his sight without turning his head.

"Please get up from the chair and lie on your stomach, Midori," Grandma requested in a voice at once firm but not unkind.

As Midori acceded to his grandmother's wishes, she pulled up the back of his shirt, took a deep breath and placed the incense on the upper part of Midori's back, and lit it. She waited for a reaction that never came.

Midori picked his way down the stone path from the front door of Grandma's house toward the river. He smiled as his favorite cherry blossom tree came into view. His steps quickened until he was running gently down the path. He grabbed the cherry blossom with his left arm and swung round and round its sturdy trunk. Eventually, Midori dropped to his knees and then lay flat on his stomach. His eyes searched the ground near the tree until he saw the small spot where the dirt was piled just a bit higher than that surrounding it. He began to burrow until he had all the earth pushed aside, and he started to pull rocks from the hole.

Every Sunday after visiting the temple, Midori placed a rock in the hole to count the weeks since Mama and George had left. He tried to count them for a while, but now there were way too many. Midori closed his eyes and conjured memories of his mother and his older brother. The contours of their faces, Mama's hair. He tried to bring back their voices as well.

As Midori lay on the ground playing with the rocks, he caught sight of a flower trying desperately to burst out of its bud. He studied the delicate yellow beauty. Its green stem swayed in the barely perceptible breeze. The stem hardly seemed strong enough for what awaited it when the weather warmed, and the flower grew ever more robust. Midori slid his frail body to the left of the flower and then to the right, taking notice of every detail, from every angle, of this new piece of wonder.

Midori suddenly became aware of an incessant screeching. He quickly pushed the rocks, save one, back into the hole, and covered them with dirt. He slipped the remaining rock into his pocket, pushed himself up on his twig-like arms, pulled his knees under him, and stood. He began trotting up the hill from the river towards the house. As he ran, Midori caught sight of Aunt Kaju off in the distance, trudging back from the cemetery. Her husband, Uncle Kumaki, had died before Midori arrived. Yet, every day since Midori's arrival she had faithfully visited his grave and tidied the area near the headstone, even when it didn't need cleaning. And, as Midori had once witnessed, she talked to her late husband.

"Everyone who sees me will know I've lost something very close and special to me," she had murmured the day Midori spied on her. Aunt Kaju was kneeling while brushing a tiny pebble from Kumaki's grave. Once she was certain the grave was clear of debris, she placed her fingertips on the spot that used to house her eyebrows. She slowly ran her fingers across the bare skin before standing and beginning the trek back to the house as Midori watched, his slight body hugging the massive tree at the border of the cemetery.

Midori snapped to attention as the source of the screeching became apparent. As he approached the house, Midori saw his older brothers, Roy and Jack, covered in mud and slapping at each other with open hands. Midori covered his ears and trotted past ignoring the boys' taunts.

As Midori approached the door he reflexively reached his hand around to the top of his back and felt the still tender, singed skin. He had wondered why Jack and Roy had scars on their back. Now he knew. They, too, had been held to account by Grandma.

Midori quickly dropped his hand and inhaled the cool, crisp air. Although the day had been unseasonably mild, the late afternoon was now enveloped in a damp chill, and Midori could smell the charcoal fire that Grandma had burning in the recessed pit in the middle of the floor.

Midori opened the door to find Grandma sitting in her usual spot hard by the fire. Her hacking cough often devolved into such a spasm that Midori sometimes wondered if her entire body might explode. Midori tiptoed past Grandma, afraid that his very presence might spark a convulsion. Grandma watched impassively as Midori opened the door to the bedroom he shared with Roy and Jack.

Midori wondered if tonight might be a "tweener." A night when the boys wouldn't know if they were to sleep in their room or if everyone would sleep in the main room for warmth. He slid onto his tatami and took the rock from his pocket. He lay on his back and turned the rock around and around, looking at it from every possible angle. Years in the riverbed had smoothed it, and it felt cool to the touch. The middle of the bottom of its oval shape had a minor dimple allowing Midori to place his thumb there as he examined it. Midori marveled at just how perfectly the rock fit in his small palm.

Midori smiled as he thought about his rock. Do rocks have parents, Midori wondered? Did his rock's mother leave him there in the river, the same way Midori's mother had left him? Midori's smile broadened. "I will adopt you," Midori promised. "You will never have to worry about being alone again." Midori patted his rock and placed it in his pocket. "I will call you, "Thumbprint," he whispered.

It didn't take long after the sun set to realize that this was not going to be a tweener. The early spring temperature dropped rapidly as Midori's brothers, three cousins, and Aunt Kaju crowded around Grandma's table eating fish soup and noodles. As the youngest, Midori had to take up residence on the floor along with his youngest cousin, Masue, since the table only sat six. He sat closest to Aunt Kaju and her two daughters, steering clear of Roy and Jack and their unseen blows to his ribs.

As Midori sat quietly eating, Jack lifted his bowl and recklessly slurped, spilling soup on the table until he finished. Grandma stared at Jack and finally spoke.

"Yoshio-san, where are your manners? Your mother will think I raised you like wolves. You are ten years old, and big for your age, too. Please act like a young man, or I will need to teach you how to do so. Remember where you come from," she continued, her voice dropping to a whisper.

Grandma adjusted her kimono and then cinched her shawl tightly over her shoulders and continued to glare at Jack while stealing glances at the others as well. She straightened her back and brought her spoon to her lips without a sound. Midori looked back at his bowl and finished the meager offerings. As soon as everyone was done eating, Midori and his cousin, Masue, who, at nine, was the second youngest, cleared the bowls and rinsed and dried them.

Midori and his brothers pulled their mats and threadbare comforters, the insides of which had found their way through their covers, into the main room. Roy helped Grandma stoke the charcoals hoping to extend their glowing life by a few minutes. But, eventually, the three brothers were forced to leave the relative warmth of their grandmother's four-room house, and head to the small, wooden hut to retrieve enough charcoal to last the night. Midori shivered as he stepped outside. It took several minutes for his eyes to acclimate to the darkness. Just as he got his footing, Jack tackled him from behind. Midori scrambled to his feet, looked at Jack, and walked away. Jack towered over Midori, so he headed to the charcoal hut, a wary eye glancing backward.

The strong charcoal scent enveloped the room once the fire was stoked. The family arranged their mats so that their feet faced the fire, and their heads were closest to the walls. A light smokiness joined the charcoal scent and pervaded their every pore.

Shortly after everyone had comfortably arranged themselves, there was a tentative knock and the door slowly opened. Akito, the family's former rickshaw driver, and Hanae, who had been Aunt Kaju's maid, entered clutching their mats.

"Please make room for our friends," Grandma requested, and the brothers scrunched together to allow Akito and Hanae to squeeze into the circle.

Grandma had reminded the boys more than once that Akito was formerly the family's full-time rickshaw driver. But, that was before Grandpa had blown through all the money on his failed business. And, before Akito's legs had become so racked with arthritis that he could no longer work. Now, if the family needed transportation, they had to hire a rickshaw driver for the trip. Friends often offered the services of their rickshaw drivers, but Grandma always waved them off.

Once, when Midori had asked Grandma why she didn't accept the offer of a rickshaw driver, she sat him on her knee, looked at him for what seemed like forever, and said, "Midori, we are Shimodas. We are descended from a proud line of Samurai. We don't need charity or handouts. Your father is in America, working very hard as a cook since jobs are so hard to come by here right now. He takes care of us, and we will one day prosper without the help of anyone outside our family, do you understand?"

Midori lay on his tatami surrounded by the others who huddled close to the fire. He glanced toward the door on the far side of the room. The one that no one ever mentioned or opened. Once when Midori came in from a trip to the river, the door was wide open, and Midori saw row upon row of medicine bottles. He had moved closer to the open door until he saw Grandma in the room arranging bottles on the shelves and dusting them off. Midori had suddenly found himself paralyzed by fear, unable to make his feet move. At that moment, Grandma had looked up before Midori could escape.

"Come in here, Midori," she motioned, her face unusually relaxed. "Sit down."

"Yes, Bachan," Midori said as he averted her eyes.

"Do you know what this room is, Midori?" Grandma asked softly.

"No, Grandma, will you tell me, please?"

"I suppose I will. Yes, Midori, I will," Grandma swayed ever so slightly as she answered. "This is a doctor's office. Your Aunt Kaju's husband, Uncle Kumaki, your father's brother, was a doctor. This was his office."

"How did he die, Bachan?" Midori asked, his eyes now locked on the older woman's.

"He drank himself to death, little one. He was an alcoholic, do you know what that is, Midori?"

"Not really," Midori admitted.

"Well, you see, there's a kind of drink that tastes good to some people. And, it makes them very happy when they drink it. But, if they drink too much of it, it can kill them. That's what happened to my son, your Uncle Kumaki. As you see, it broke poor Kaju's heart. She can barely take care of her children now." Grandma suddenly caught Midori's eye. "It broke my heart, too, little one. It broke my heart too," she sniffed.

Midori watched his grandmother and nodded his understanding.

"Come now, enough," Grandma suddenly intoned, and just like that they were out of the office. Midori never saw that room again, and Grandma never again spoke of Uncle Kumaki.

Morning came in a hurry, and when Midori awoke, he could see his breath. The fire had long since died, and only the warmth from eight other human bodies kept him from freezing on his mat. Midori looked around and quickly realized he was the first one awake, which wasn't all that unusual. He pulled his tatami aside, stood softly, and picked his way among the sleeping bodies littering the floor until he reached the door. Midori picked up the box used to carry the charcoal and headed for the hut. The ground was rock hard, and the frost permeated what remained of the soles on his shoes.

The still visible morning moon glinted off the frostbitten trees causing Midori to stop in his tracks. He looked with bemusement as the light danced off the topmost branches. While the morning seemed still at Midori's height, the uppermost branches swayed, lending an otherworldliness to the dawn. Midori stood, transfixed until he heard the front door open.

"Hey, squirt, you planning on getting charcoal or just staring at the treetops?" Roy was shivering, and Midori could see behind him that the others were as well. He trotted over to the charcoal hut and filled the box to the top. But, he wasn't strong enough to lift it. He alternately pushed and pulled the container, its wooden bottom occasionally catching on the ground and sending him sprawling. Roy watched from the door, shaking his head.

Midori got the charcoal carrier within a foot or so of the door when Roy stepped out, grabbed the box, and announced to the others, "okay, we finally have some charcoal. Excuse me, so that I can get us all warm again."

This morning the charcoal did double duty, heating both the room and the water on the stove. Breakfast consisted of a piece of dry, salty fish and some hot tea.

Midori took his time drinking his tea. As a reward for having fetched the charcoal, Grandma offered Midori extra hot water when he finished, and he gladly accepted it. After the mats were rolled up and the table and chairs wiped clean, Grandma warmed more water for the boys and their cousins to use to wash. It was Sunday. Shortly, they would all leave for the temple to pray for Midori's father in America. The father he'd never met.

"Let's go now, everyone," Grandma insisted. "Makeo-san, Yoshio-san, and Midori-san, you will be with me. Masue-san, Masae-san, and Hisao-san, please get in the back rickshaw.

Midori and Jack helped Grandma into the rickshaw as the driver steadied himself. Grandma arranged her kimono, and the boys took their seats.

Midori watched the driver pick up the rickshaw, his sinewy arms straining under the burden. Slowly, the rickshaw moved forward. Midori noticed the driver's labored breathing and wondered if he should offer to help. But, the driver was mostly quiet, only occasionally calling out to the other driver to co-ordinate their respective paces. Besides, Midori knew that he couldn't pull the rickshaw. Still, he worried about the man tasked with doing so.

The morning was chilly despite the warm sun. Midori sat firmly upright in the seat to the far right of Grandma. By now, the ritual and the scenery it revealed were quite familiar. The sun was behind Midori, so he watched the driver's shadow dancing in front of him, leading the way. Midori glanced at the trees whose branches had just enough of a green glow to hint at leaves and the coming spring.

An hour later, the temple came into view. It was shiny and golden, and the mid-morning sunshine glinted off its dome, which seemed to Midori to tower endlessly toward the sky. There were several other rickshaws parked in front to the left of the door as the family's two drivers came to a stop. Roy and Jack stepped down from the rickshaw and turned to help Grandma. Midori waited his turn and then hopped down and headed to the other rickshaw to help Aunt Kaju alight. The family re-connected, and Grandma led the way into the front door.

Once inside, the bright early morning sunshine was but a memory. Midori waited for his eyes to acclimate and then took note that the others had wandered on ahead. Midori knew where to find them. On the left side of the vast main room was a separate room with a low-slung ceiling from which hung dozens upon dozens of wooden legs, each with a special carving.

Jack quietly approached Midori. "Hey, little man, any new wooden legs in here?"

Midori scanned the room and began inching towards the far left corner. The windowless space was dank, despite the warming day, and was only lit by a few small, bare bulbs. Midori fixed his gaze above him on the wooden legs hanging from a metal strand that stretched across the better part of the room before hooking into the wall. Some of the wooden legs appeared to be those of adults, while others were quite small. Midori studied them all as Jack stared at his little brother.

Finally, Midori pointed up toward a non-descript wooden leg with virtually no carvings. "Here," he said, "This one is new. It was not here last week."

As Jack stared up at the leg Midori had pointed out, Grandma approached. "Have you boys prayed for your father's health? For the recovery of *his* leg?"

"Yes, Bachan," Jack lied.

14

"No, Bachan," Midori said evenly. "I am sorry I will do so now." With that, Midori walked swiftly away from Grandma and Jack and entered the main room. He approached the large altar in the middle of the room, knelt and prayed for the return to health of the father whose appearance he could only try to conjure in his mind's eye.

JACK, ROY, MIDORI AND GEORGE – KUMAMOTO C. 1913

CHAPTER THREE

The Africa Maru

September 1919

September 21st began as most every other early fall day in Kumamoto. The sun rose behind Grandma's house, and the dew tickled the grass and trees. Midori awoke and dressed quickly, downing a cup of tea before waiting to see if Jack and Roy would be joining him and going to school since they both had been coughing all morning. He wasn't even slightly surprised when Bachan admonished them both to have a quiet day, then sent the three boys on their way.

A few short hours later, as Grandma sat quietly in her favorite chair, there was a knock on the door, which swung open before Grandma could alight.

"Setsuo-san!" Grandma called out as she hugged her eldest grandson. "Oh my, how grown-up you are! Oh, and who is this?" she smiled and hugged her daughter-in-law tightly.

Grandma updated Mama Shimoda and her oldest son, who had changed his name to George once he moved to America, about Roy, Jack, and Midori as they sipped hot tea. Then she asked about her son's leg.

"Papa is much better, thankfully. We know you have been praying at the temple every Sunday, and the prayers were answered. We are so grateful," Mama Shimoda explained. "We are also so grateful to you for watching the boys these years to ground them in our traditions and values before they become surrounded by life in America. It would not have been possible if we'd had them all to look after."

"Ah, that is very good to hear," Grandma smiled. Then, her tone solemn, she asked, "I suppose you are here to take Roy, Jack, and Midori back to America, then?"

"Yes, I am so sorry, but, yes, we are," Mama Shimoda replied, barely able to meet her mother-in-law's gaze.

"I understand," said Grandma, her head bowed ever so slightly. "I will miss your brothers a great deal," she said as she faced George, "but," she continued and pointed to Mama Shimoda, "their place is with their mother and father. In America, with you. Yes, this is the right thing, even if it hurts to say so."

"We will head to Yokohama to the ship tomorrow," George explained. "The Africa Maru sails on the 27th, and it will take several days for us to get to Yokohama. We will sail to America together. All five of us."

Grandma looked directly at her eldest grandson, her impassive face betraying absolutely no emotion. Then, she fixed her gaze on her daughter-in-law. Eventually, she stood and walked to the window where she brushed away a tear and gently ran her fingers through her silvery hair.

As the afternoon sun shone brightly on the front of Grandma's house, the three younger boys burst through the door searching for a snack. Midori was the first to see his brother, George, and it stopped him in his tracks. His eyes scanned the room. He ran to George, then suddenly stopped, just shy of him. George grabbed Midori in a bear hug.

"Midori," he smiled. "Are you eating? Doesn't Bachan feed you?"

Midori blushed as Jack and Roy crowded around their big brother.

"You two must be stealing Midori's food!" George smiled.

"Is Mama here?" Midori murmured.

"Turn around, Midori-san," George smiled.

Midori turned and saw his mother waiting with open arms. It had been over three years since she'd left him without even so much as a goodbye. He stood, not quite knowing what to do. But, Mama Shimoda ran towards her little boy and hugged him deeply, not letting go for many minutes.

Midori wiped away more than a few tears as Roy and Jack jockeyed for time with Mama. Eventually, Midori allowed Mama Shimoda to pull away so his brothers could bathe in her warmth.

Soon the talk turned to the upcoming trip.

"How, how will we go?" Jack asked, stifling a cough.

"By boat," George replied. "A big ship called the Africa Maru. It will take several weeks for us to get to Seattle."

The questions poured forth. How many people would be on the boat? What would they eat? Where would they sleep? Where exactly is Seattle? Eventually, the three younger boys began to run out of steam. Finally, Midori looked at Grandma.

"Grandma, can you come to America with us?" he asked.

Grandma smiled, put her arm around Midori's tiny shoulders, and shook her head.

It was late at night when Mama Shimoda and the boys finally made it to Yokohama. George found a rooming house that bordered somewhere between seedy and economical. He was able to secure beds for Mama as well as himself and his three brothers.

Midori lay on his back and tried to close his eyes, but Jack's coughing kept startling him awake. The others slept peacefully before they all awoke early to the sound of ship horns, and the bustle of the harbor.

The room was windowless, so Midori lay awake, staring at the ceiling and awaiting direction from George. Midori noticed that there were small cracks in the ceiling, and he traced them with his eyes from one corner the next. He was following a tiny, tender looking fissure when Mama urged the boys to all get up and get dressed.

The late September sky was clear, the air crisp, as Mama and the boys made their way towards the docks. The Africa Maru rose from the water, docked between several other large ships, its gray steel hull simultaneously imposing and non-descript.

The faded white, clapboard administration building stood to the left, and Mama helped George guide the three younger boys there for the check-in before their journey. George approached the uniformed man behind the small desk and handed him a swatch of papers. The man, whose nameplate gave away that he was called "Mr. Kumimoto" rifled through the papers, and then looked up.

"Okay," Mr. Kumimoto smiled, "you all need to wait over there," he motioned. "All of you need medical exams to make certain you're healthy and strong enough to make the trip to America and for the Americans to let you into their country. Otherwise, your papers are in order."

Midori glanced around the waiting room. It had several chairs, most of which were taken by senior citizens with sad, drawn faces. A group of pretty, young women stood in a separate corner from the family, giggling and whispering. As the boys waited, Midori suddenly heard a slap, followed rapidly by Roy's high-pitched cackle. Jack was holding his hand to his cheek, an incredulous look on his face.

"You're in big trouble, you loser," Jack screamed. But, before he could retaliate, George grabbed Jack's arm and twisted it be-

21

hind his back. Jack's face was the definition of shock as he tried to squirm away and cried out, "George, that jerk of a brother started it! I was just standing here."

Before Mama could even react, George responded. "I understand, Jack, now stand still, and I'll let you go. But, don't even think of starting anything with Roy, or *I* will make *both* of you very sorry. We need to be calm for our medical exams."

One by one, first Mama, and then the boys disappeared behind the door on the left side of the cramped waiting room as they were called for their exams. Midori was the last to emerge, and he handed George the slip of paper the nice lady had given to him after his examination.

George looked grim. "Midori is the only one of us who passed the medical exam," he said, shaking his head. "We," he motioned toward Mama Shimoda, Jack, and Roy, "will need to stay in Yokohama until our conditions improve, and then we will sail to America too. I think what happened to Mama and me is we got colds on the ship over. Jack, you have a cold too, they only need to listen to your cough. Roy, they said you had a low-grade fever as well. Do you feel okay?"

Roy nodded vigorously as George and Mama huddled a few feet away.

"I would have passed if Roy hadn't slapped me!" Jack screamed. "The nurse kept asking me about the red mark on my cheek. She was worried I had a skin disease or something!"

"Wait," Midori cried out, "what does this mean? I will wait with you until all of you pass, right?"

Mama looked to a spot past Midori and didn't respond as George furrowed his brow and shrugged before heading over to the desk for a conversation with Mr. Kumimoto. George returned quickly with his hands thrust in his pockets, and his lips held tightly together.

"Midori, your test results are only good for the upcoming trip today. If you wait with us, you will need to be examined again. You could catch a cold from one of us, and then, you could fail. We can't take that chance."

The color drained from Midori's face as his older brothers stood quietly with Mama. "You're lucky," Jack said, tapping Midori's arm. "In a few weeks, you will be with Papa in America, while we're stuck here."

George glanced gratefully at Jack and nodded his agreement. "And we will meet you there as soon as we can. Meantime, let's all give Midori our food, so he's not hungry."

The boys and Mama quickly rifled through their food packs and began handing packages to Midori, who unwrapped the cloth, which held his food. As Midori added the extra food to what he was already carrying and re-wrapped it, his lower lip trembled, and he turned towards Mama. He started to speak, but then abruptly stopped. Finally, he whispered, "when do I leave?'

George gestured toward the door, "now, little one, we'll walk with you to the ramp," he said as Mama watched in silence.

Midori looked over his shoulder at his brothers and Mama,

all of whom waved to him. He carried his small suitcase and his tightly wrapped cloth, which, in addition to food, was full of underwear, kimono, and shirts. He quickly was swallowed up by his fellow travelers, most of whom were young women headed to America for marriage. The Japanese men who were to become their husbands had chosen their soon to be wives solely by seeing their pictures.

Midori glanced from side to side every so often but mostly kept his focus straight ahead, taking two steps for everyone else's one, as he tried to keep up. Every few seconds, he would run several steps to try to keep pace, though there was a large crowd behind him, and he was in no danger of being left behind. His stomach churned as the emptiness grew. In his mind's eye, he could still see Mama as she waved to him, which was more than she did the last time she abandoned him.

Midori eventually settled himself on the floor near the center of the back of the big ship. Young women surrounded him, all giggling and twirling their hair. Midori leaned against his suitcase and propped himself up with his left elbow. In his right hand, he held Thumbprint. He turned the smooth rock over and over in his hand, a smile curling the corner of his lips.

"Ticket!" the man in the drab gray uniform demanded, his stiff arm outstretched. Midori fished around in his pocket until he found a slightly crumpled paper. He began to reach up from his perch when the man snatched the ticket from him and peered at it. "Below!" he snapped as he gestured towards the steps. Midori scrambled to his feet, clutching his cloth and his small, worn suitcase. He began walking toward the stairs glancing back over his shoulder every few seconds to see if the ticket man was following him.

The metal steps were slippery, and Midori held tightly to the railing as he headed down. As he descended, the air thickened noticeably. Upon reaching the lower deck, Midori surveyed his new quarters. To his left was an area that held an array of luggage along with boxed food and tea bags. Moisture gathered on the outside of the boxes staining each in a way that made them look like unique, hand-painted masterpieces. Midori traced each one with his eyes, smiling ever so slightly.

Midori made his way past the boxes and began to settle into a hidden corner. He propped up his wrapped cloth and leaned against it. For the first time since boarding, Midori felt pangs of hunger. But, they didn't compare with the pangs of loneliness and longing he felt. He pulled Thumbprint from his pocket and held it tightly in his right hand.

His stiff neck told Midori that he'd been asleep for some time, but, in truth, he had no real idea how long. The lower deck was dark, but Midori could see some fading light from the stairwell. He sat up, rubbed his eyes, and yawned.

"Good morning," laughed the young woman hovering over Midori. "What's your name?"

"I am Midori," came the soft reply.

The woman knelt and smiled again. Midori could smell something sweet as she put her face close to his. "I am Aiko," she said as she desperately tried to hold Midori's gaze. "Are you traveling alone?"

Midori nodded and whispered, "My mama and brothers were too sick to travel so they sent me to go meet Papa."

"Do you have food for the trip?"

Midori nodded. "I have some rice balls and some slices of pickled daikon radish. Grandma gave it to me. Oh, I also have extra that Mama and my brothers gave me."

"How many rice balls?" Aiko asked, her voice rising.

Midori thought for a moment. "I don't know. A couple, for my-self, probably another eight or ten from my brothers and Mama, why?"

"This crossing will take close to three weeks. You will need more than ten or twelve rice balls!"

◆ ◆ ◆

How many more days until we get to America?" Midori asked Aiko. The young woman had secured a spot on the main deck for herself and Midori, and he hadn't left her side since.

"The captain says one more week. Seven days more, little one," Aiko smiled.

Midori clung to the young woman's dress with his left hand and looked up to her with wide eyes. "Do you think your husband will be waiting for you when you arrive?" he asked.

"I certainly hope so! We have seen pictures of each other. I hope I can recognize him!" Aiko grinned while biting the corner of her lip. "There will be many, many men at the docks, little one. "I'm going to look for the one with the best smile and just hope he's the one!"

"Well,' Midori giggled, "I think my dad will be the biggest, strongest and best-looking man on the dock, but he will call for me, so you will know that he's not your husband."

Aiko smirked and rubbed Midori's head. "Yes, that's right. I can tell by looking at you that your dad will be handsome. Maybe not that tall, but handsome."

"My brother, George, is very tall! My other brothers are kind of tall too. I think one day I will be tall too; it's just taking a while for it to happen. I'm not even ten yet!"

Aiko rubbed Midori's head again, and he smiled, but quickly looked away. "Let's get something to eat," Aiko suggested, as she glanced towards Midori. "You seem very quiet today, little one," she said.

Midori stopped walking and looked at Aiko. "I, I guess I'm a little sad today, Aiko. I'm so very sorry."

"No need to apologize, Midori," Aiko replied, her eyes betraying her affection for her young charge. "We all get sad sometimes."

"I only get sad when I miss Mama," Midori responded, holding onto Thumbprint with one hand and grasping Aiko's hand with his other one.

PORTION OF MIDORI'S IMMIGRATION DOCUMENT – SEPTEMBER
1919

CHAPTER FOUR

Seattle, Washington

October 1919-June 1920

Midori clutched the cinched-up cloth and his suitcase together in his right hand. He held Aiko's hand with his left. Aiko kept jumping up and down, trying to gain a better sightline as the ship steamed into Seattle harbor. Midori couldn't see beyond the swell of squealing young women who pressed up against the front railing. Still more women screamed behind Midori and pressed forward, almost crushing the little boy. Midori squeezed Aiko's hand, and she smiled down at him, her body quivering with the excitement of the ship's arrival.

Aiko reached down, wrapped her arms around Midori, and lifted him above the pulsing mass of women. He scanned the dozens of faces on the dock.

"There he is!" Midori called out and pointed toward the father he'd never seen. "I know it, that's him!" Midori squirmed out of Aiko's arms and began to slither his way through the squealing women. Suddenly, he stopped and found his way back to Aiko. He grabbed her hand. "Thank you for everything, Aiko," the little boy smiled. I will never forget you!"

Aiko hugged Midori tightly, and then she patted him on the head. "Go, little one, find your dad!" And, with that, he was off.

Midori picked his way through the picture brides who took turns primping and giggling. He held his wrapped cloth and suitcase tightly and alternated between letting the crowd pull him forward and making his way more quickly. Finally, he was off the ship. He turned to his left in the direction of the man he knew, just knew, to be his father.

Just as quickly as Midori had seen the man, the crowd swallowed him up. Midori's heart raced as he pressed forward. Japanese men held photographs in their hands as they scoured the hordes of women exiting the ship. They all ignored the little boy as he scampered along. Reaching an open area, Midori found a bench where an elderly woman was sitting. He climbed up next to her and stood on his toes peering from side to side while rubbing Thumbprint.

As Midori continued trying to find his father, he felt a gentle hand on his left shoulder. "Hello, Midori," came the sonorous voice. "It's nice to meet you, my son."

"Hello, father," Midori smiled before looking down at his shoes. "I'm so very pleased to meet you," he continued as Papa lifted him in a huge bear hug.

Midori took one final glance over his shoulder, hoping to locate Aiko, but she was gone, in search of her new life in America.

"Papa," Midori said shyly as the large man gently placed him back on the ground, "how will we get to your house?"

Papa took Midori's hand and slowly walked so the little boy

could keep up. "Midori-san, it's our house, not my house," he smiled. "And I came here on my bicycle. It may be a bit tricky, but we will ride it back together."

"Is it far from here, Papa?"

"Not so far, little one," Papa replied squeezing, his son's hand. "We will have an easy ride, and then I will show you your new home and the room where you will sleep."

Papa climbed up onto his black and silver bike and motioned for Midori to place his things in the front basket. Midori crammed his suitcase in the basket, but there was no room for his tightly wrapped cloth. Papa partially untied the cloth and re-tied it around Midori's arm before helping his son climb onto the handlebars.

As father and son made their way through town, Midori marveled at the buildings and all of the different looking people. Not only were many of them Caucasian, but they all seemed so tall! Papa pointed out various landmarks to Midori and eventually slowed before coming to a stop in front of a small, box-like house with a tiny porch framing the entrance.

"Welcome to your new home, Midori," Papa smiled as he got off the bike.

Midori slid off the handlebars, grabbed his suitcase from the basket, and followed Papa inside. He was immediately drawn to a picture on the wall that he recognized as being his grandma. The house was mostly clean though Papa smiled when he showed the room he shared with Mama to Midori.

"Midori-san," Papa laughed, "you must promise not to tell Mama that I don't make the bed when she is not here!"

Papa ruffled his son's hair as Midori leaned against his father's muscular leg.

The morning after Midori arrived, Papa introduced him to Mrs. Nagano, the short, round-faced lady who lived next door. For the next few weeks, Mrs. Nagano arrived every weekday morning at 8:15 and helped Midori off to his new school. Midori learned that he and Papa lived in a part of town known as Japantown. All of their immediate neighbors were Japanese, as were the boys and girls in Midori's new school.

Midori spent his first few weeks in America going to class, and then exploring Japantown with Mrs. Nagano after school ended each day. The area was compact and easily traversed, and Midori quickly began to recognize the various shops. Mrs. Nagano took him to her favorite Japanese grocery stores and showed him many other small, Japanese owned businesses, including his new favorite, Mr. Shinjo's candy store. The daily trips through Japantown had the curious effect of both lessening and heightening Midori's feelings of homesickness.

Because he didn't speak English, Midori was put in first grade, despite being nine and a half years old. He quickly learned English, which lessened the bullying and taunting he initially faced. The transition eased further when Mama, George, Roy, and Jack arrived from Japan. The three older boys slept in a small bedroom directly off the kitchen. Midori had his own bedroom for what he knew would be a very short time, since immediately adjacent to his tiny bed was a wooden crib. His roommate would make an appearance in the not too distant future, of that Midori was certain.

One misty, late Fall night, Midori awoke to a cacophony of foreign sounds. There were voices he didn't recognize, and Mama was crying out at ever decreasing intervals. Midori crept to the door and tried to peek out, but the room was crowded with adults, and he couldn't quite make out what was happening. Climbing back into bed, Midori pulled out Thumbprint and rolled the smooth rock around in his right hand. He switched it to his left hand and rubbed it with more intention as the screaming from his mother reached a fevered pitch. And then, just like that, his mother's screaming stopped, there was cheering and then a tiny little cry.

The next morning Midori peeked out of his door and saw several adults sleeping on the floor. Papa was in the corner near the stove boiling water for tea. Midori took a few steps, stopped to survey the room, and then continued in.

"Ah, Midori-san," Papa called out with a smile. "Come out. You have a new sister! We are calling her 'Setsuko'," Papa continued as he reached to hug Midori. "Good news, Midori-san. You are no longer the littlest Shimoda!"

"Papa-san, can I see Setsuko?" Midori asked his eyes fixed on his father's face.

"Not now, little one. Setsuko and Mama are sleeping. But, soon, my son, soon, I promise."

George, Roy, and Jack broke the early morning peace by crowding into the kitchen together. Just as George began to speak,

Roy smacked the back of Jack's head. As Jack turned to retaliate, Papa Shimoda grabbed Jack's hand. "Back in the bedroom you two until you are ready to behave," Papa said sternly.

George took notice of the other adults in the room who were in varying states of wakefulness. "Oh!" he cried out, "do we have a brother or a sister?"

Papa smiled broadly. "You finally have a sister. We are calling her 'Setsuko'," Papa gestured toward the bedroom. "She's asleep with Mama-san. It was a long night."

◆ ◆ ◆

Every night, Mama would tiptoe into Midori's room and pick up Setsuko as soon as she started to whimper. Sometimes Midori would awaken after Mama was already there. Some nights Mama would sit quietly with Setsuko on her chest. Other nights, Mama would take her out of the room.

As the cold and rainy Winter gave way to a lush green Spring, Mama's nighttime visits became less frequent. Most nights, Set-suko would sleep all the way through. Midori didn't know what a bad baby might act like, but he knew that Setsuko was a good baby. A very good baby, as Mama said over and over again.

It was a late Sunday afternoon in early June when the sun seemed to linger forever in the western sky. Midori came inside after a long walk that eventually had taken him down towards and into the woods a few blocks from the Shimoda home. Two new boarding house tenants had recently moved in, and Papa Shimoda was back, at least temporarily, from his job working on the ferry. As Midori entered through the back door, he could feel the walls closing in on him. There was a warmth in the tiny house, but it was crammed and smothering too.

Midori removed his zori sandals and placed them just inside the back door. He patted Setsuko's head as the toddler scooted along the floor on all fours. To his left, Midori spied Mama and walked over to kiss her cheek. Mama looked up from her handiwork, "hello, Midori-san, what have you been doing my son?"

"I was down near the woods, Mama. I saw a beautiful tree. I want to ask Papa what kind of tree it is."

"Papa walked down to the store to get some things I need to make dinner. He and George will be back soon. You can ask him then, little one," Mama smiled.

"What are you making now, Mama? You always seem to be working on something."

"I am making gloves, Midori-san. Papa will sell them once I am done. Then, I will start on another pair. The men on the ferry love my gloves! At least that's what Papa tells me." Mama's eyes twinkled as she spoke.

Mama boiled up a mixture of green vegetables, onions, and, this being Sunday, salmon. The family gathered around the table to eat, but it wasn't easy for everyone to fit with Papa, four boys, one girl, and Mama.

As soon as dinner ended, Papa stood. He gestured to the three older boys. "You three, please clean up from dinner. Mama-san cooked, and she needs to sit down now. "Midori-san, come with me."

Midori quickly scrambled to his feet and followed a foot or so behind Papa. When they got outside the house, Papa picked up the gas lantern and lit it. "Mama told me that there is a tree you would like me to see. Show me where it is."

Midori trotted along next to Papa, who took one step to the little boy's three. Midori pressed his hand into his pocket, tightly grasping Thumbprint as he struggled to keep up.

"This way, Papa," Midori called out, his feet barely grazing the ground as he swung to his left and headed towards the woods. As they approached the woods, Midori began to sprint as Papa laughed and loped along with the lantern swinging back and forth.

Midori turned around to see the light from the lantern glancing off of his father's weathered hands. Midori noticed a spot on Papa's left hand where the skin appeared to be peeling. There was an angry red patch on the outer edge of the older man's palm.

"Papa," Midori suddenly stopped in his tracks. "Does your hand hurt?"

Papa rubbed Midori's head and smiled. "No, my son, it's fine. Sometimes we lift rough packages on the ferry, and they cut our hands. It's just part of the job, Midori-san. Now, where is your tree?"

Midori ran along the edge of the woods and stopped, pointing at a small tree with wispy, fragile deep red leaves.

"Ah, Midori-san, that's a Japanese Maple. Do you remember ever seeing one back in Japan?"

Midori tugged at his left ear and then scratched his forehead as he wrinkled his nose. After a long period of thought he said, "no, Papa, I'm sorry, I don't remember ever seeing one before."

"Oh, that's okay, my son, I just thought it might be a memory from Japan."

"Is this a baby tree, Papa?"

"It looks young, Midori-san, but I don't think it's a baby tree. Japanese Maple can grow fairly large, maybe 20 feet high. This one looks to be, oh, maybe five feet tall so far. They can grow straight up, like these other trees," Papa explained, gesturing at the Douglas Fir evergreens populating the majority of the woods. "Or," he continued, "they can grow more widely, more broadly, their leaves covering much of the grass underneath." This time Papa spread his hands out in front of him, palms down, hands together. Then, he slowly pulled them away from each other, turned his palms inward and turned both hands at equal, but opposite right angles and moved them toward the ground.

Midori watched his father's hands as they traced the outline of an imaginary Japanese Maple. He took in every word that

Papa spoke and slowly nodded his understanding. When Papa stopped speaking, Midori walked up to the Japanese Maple and caressed its leaves. He and Papa stood in silence for a bit before Papa indicated with a swing of the lantern that it was time to return home.

CHAPTER FIVE

Bremerton, Washington

July 1920

Midori methodically filled his basket with strawberries. When it was filled to the top Midori tried to pick it up, but he couldn't. Next, he tried to push it. That didn't work either. So, he was left with no choice but to remove some strawberries from his basket and place them in another boy's basket.

"Look, Squirt can't lift his basket," cackled one of the bigger boys. "How old are you, six?" the boy taunted.

"He can't even push it!" chimed in another.

Midori squinted at his tormentors, making a mental note of their faces and expressions. He didn't bother telling them that he was ten.

The boy to whom Midori gave his strawberries was almost as small as Midori. He nodded but said nothing as Midori kept emptying his basket, a few strawberries at a time, until he was finally able to lift the basket and take it to the counting room.

"What is your name, little one?" the man in the room asked, arching his head skyward.

"Midori," came the reply.

The man stopped and looked down. "Do you have a family name, son, that would help me to make sure you get paid?"

"My family name is Shimoda," Midori replied, his eyes firmly fixed upon the floor directly beneath him.

"I hope you get better at this, son, or you won't make much money!"

Midori headed back out, the empty basket balancing on his head as he scampered to his picking area. He began looking around for the spot where he'd been, but it appeared to be picked clean. He glanced from side to side and saw the bigger boys picking away. Many of them had strawberry juice staining their hands and faces. Two rows to the left, a fight was brewing, so Midori quickly turned and headed right. Eventually, he found a row that seemed to have enough strawberries to make it worthwhile to stay.

As soon as he started to pick, Midori felt the presence of another. He turned to his left to see the young boy into whose basket he'd placed the strawberries he couldn't carry. Midori nodded at the boy, and they began to pick in silence. When Midori's basket was about one-quarter filled, his new friend put his hand on Midori's shoulder.

"Please," said the boy. "Wait." With that, the boy began taking strawberries from his basket and placing them gently in Midori's basket.

"Oh, no!" cried Midori. "Please, you don't need to do that. It's very kind of you, but I will pick my own. Thank you."

◆ ◆ ◆

Bremerton, Washington

July 1921

Midori headed straight for the shed. If anything, it looked dustier than the prior summer--the stench of rotting fruit combined with just a touch of sweat to form an unforgettable miasma. Midori caught his breath and headed inside. He searched for an unoccupied bed and found that the one he'd slept in the prior summer was vacant. He hesitated a moment, then placed his cloth full of shirts, underwear, and trousers on the mattress. He folded back the covers to indicate that he was going to occupy the mattress, and he headed out to the fields.

With his basket half full, Midori briefly stopped picking strawberries. He tried, to no avail, to lift it. Next, he got in front of the basket, bent slightly from his knees, and pulled it. With little problem this time Midori, reached the counting room.

"Hello Mr. Fujimoto," Midori said, as he entered the room. "Here is my first basket."

"Ah, Midori, welcome back." The older man nodded as he appraised Midori. "All the other boys, they have grown since last summer. You don't seem any bigger to me. Does your mama feed you, little one?"

Midori smiled and backed out of the counting room in silence.

In two weeks' time, Midori had picked more strawberries than any of the other boys, despite the fact that some of them had been there much longer than he had.

"Midori, come on over here and join us for a minute," one of the older boys called out. Midori stopped picking and walked over to where the boys were sitting and smoking hand-rolled cigarettes.

"Yes?" Midori said.

"Take a break, relax. You're making the rest of us look bad. Besides, why do you have a girl's name? Did your parents think you were a girl when you were born? That would explain a lot."

The boys all laughed, and one of the taller ones made a point of tousling Midori's hair. Midori watched him as he leaned over. The boys' eyes were anything but playful. Without changing the expression on his face, Midori headed back to his basket. The strawberries he'd picked were gone. He noticed a few on the ground nearby, but the rest had been removed from his basket and pilfered. Midori picked up his basket, moved over an aisle, and resumed picking.

CHAPTER SIX

Seattle, Washington

September 1925

Midori gazed intently toward the front of the classroom; his eyes fixed on Miss Mayan. She was tall, and her long, thin hair only served to accentuate that fact. She had a warm smile that was even more fully realized when she pronounced the names of her Japanese students. Eventually, she neared the back of the alphabet.

"Midori Shimoda?" she asked, her eyes searching room.

"Present, Miss Mayan," Midori responded as he raised his hand slowly, but firmly.

"I have taught many of your brothers, Midori," Miss Mayan smiled. "I'm looking forward to teaching you as well."

"Thank you, Miss Mayan," Midori smiled before averting his gaze.

Miss Mayan completed attendance and a few other administrative matters and then led a discussion that, not surprisingly, revolved around the students' summer vacations and jobs. After some time, it was Midori's turn.

"For the summer, I went to a place called Ketchikan, which is in Alaska,' Midori explained.

"I remember that George, Jack, and Roy all spent their summers logging. Is that what you did in Ketchikan, Midori?"

"No, Miss Mayan. I worked in the salmon cannery. I cleaned the fish and sent them for chopping up and canning. Even though I am fifteen, I think I am still too small for the logging camps."

"What did you think of the cannery work, Midori?"

"It was okay. I was able to save most of the money I made to bring home to Mama and Papa to help us buy food."

"Were there other boys your age there, Midori?" Miss Mayan continued.

"Yes, there were some, and one was even shorter than I am!" Midori beamed.

Miss Mayan smiled broadly. "Thank you for sharing Midori!"

Immediately after school, Midori headed down to the Times Square building at 5th Avenue and Olive Way. In the basement of the newspaper building, there were stacks of the Seattle Daily Times bound together by heavy twine in packages containing 25 copies each. The paper was only between four and eight pages each day, so Midori was able to hoist three bundles into his pouch and head out for his daily delivery route, which consisted of 70-75 residences. Most of the deliveries were to apartments in Japantown, meaning that they were close together, but required a fair amount of stair climbing.

Midori took a deep breath and headed up the stairs for his final deliveries of the day. Right on cue, Mrs. Mayoki opened her door. "Come in, little one," she said, holding the door open.

"Mrs. Mayoki, good afternoon. I need to deliver the rest of my papers to my customers. They are waiting for them," Midori explained.

"Tsk, tsk, little one, I just need a bit of help. It won't take you but a minute."

Midori nodded and followed the tiny, bent over woman into her dark apartment. Before he knew it, Midori was standing on a small step stool, reaching up toward the top shelf of a cabinet and handing Mrs. Mayoki musty hand towels. It seemed as though there was a never-ending supply of the ancient, threadbare items. Midori began to work more quickly as he thought about his customers.

"I am an old woman, Midori, please slow down, I can't move that fast," Mrs. Mayoki snapped, wagging her gnarled index finger.

"I'm sorry, Mrs. Mayoki; I didn't mean to make it difficult for you," Midori murmured.

The second he pulled the last damp rag from the shelf, Midori climbed down and headed for the door.

"No, thank you, Mrs. Mayoki," Midori called over his shoulder in answer to the old woman's offer of a glass of water. Midori slipped out the door and hurriedly finished his deliveries before heading back to the Times Square building to pick up his schoolbooks.

Upon arriving at the building, Midori retrieved his books, took a swig of water, and began the trek home.

"Midori," a voice called out from across the street.

"Sam!" Midori responded. "What are you doing here?" he asked his best friend.

"My mom needed me to get some vegetables," Sam indicated, patting the bag he was carrying. "How was the paper route today? Did Mrs. Mayoki invite you in again?"

Midori glanced up at the taller boy and smiled. "What do you think, Sam, old boy?"

"She sounds creepy," Sam cried out before devolving into laughter.

The boys walked along together, content in each other's company. Although they were within months of each other age-wise, Sam towered over Midori.

As Sam reached his house, Midori swiped his hand on his friend's back. "Okay, Sammy, Sam, see you tomorrow!"

The tall, rail thin boy smiled and swiped back at his small friend. "Tomorrow, Midori-san."

The following morning, Midori walked off toward school in the company of his two walking companions.

"Midori," Tinky said, with a sly look. "Remember when you were stupid in first grade?"

Midori shook his head at his pudgy friend. "Remember when you were nice to me?" Midori smiled. "I'm not stupid anymore, Tinky, am I?"

"You were never stupid, Midori!" Kazuko cried out. "You just didn't know English, and you were so small!"

"He's still small," Tinky replied.

The three friends walked along toward school, easily bantering the entire way. "Midori, why do you try to play basketball?" Tinky asked.

Midori shrugged. "I don't understand that question, Tinky. Why would I not play? Why do you do anything you do? Because you like it? Because it's fun?"

Tinky stopped in his tracks. "Midori, that's the longest I've ever heard you talk at one time!"

"Yes, Midori, what came over you?" Kazuko teased.

Midori smiled but didn't respond. As they approached the school, Midori looked up to see the Beppu brothers heading his way in quite a rush. Taft was about to sideswipe Midori, but Midori was too quick and stepped aside while watching Taft barrel into Tinky.

"Hey!" screamed Tinky. "Why'd you hit me?"

"I was trying to hit the shrimp, but he moved at the last second," Taft explained.

"You're just dumb, Taft!" Tinky continued. "Why do you need to hit anyone?" Tinky asked as he pushed the pudgy boy out of the way.

Midori looked up to see Taft's twin brothers, Lincoln and Grant, laughing at the fracas. The older boys caught Midori's eye, and the three exchanged knowing glances. Midori quietly separated himself from the growing pack and headed through the door. It was another beautiful September day. Midori took one final glance at the sunshine, breathed deeply, and headed toward Miss Mayan's class.

September became October, and, as it always does, November followed. The sunlight hours decreased little by little, and the gentle rain became more insistent as Fall grudgingly gave way to Winter. Before long, Christmas was upon Seattle and its cheerful inhabitants.

A few days before the holiday, Midori took a bit of the money he'd saved from his paper route and headed out to Shinjo's, his favorite candy and toy shop. After picking through the myriad items on display, he found a small purple, plastic trinket for his mother. He picked it up and scrutinized it carefully. After assuring himself of its value, he turned to Mr. Shinjo.

"How much for this, please?"

"How much do you have Midori?" the man asked, gently placing his hand on the boy's shoulder.

Midori emptied some coins from his pocket. "I have five cents, Mr. Shinjo," he nodded with assurance.

When Mr. Shinjo smiled, the wrinkles on his face became even more pronounced. And, his already red cheeks seemed to flush just a touch more as well. "Hmm, let me look at the price, Midori," he said, tousling the boy's hair. "Well, the price tag here on the bottom says six cents. Is this a Christmas gift, Midori?"

Midori nodded, his lower lip quivering ever so slightly.

"Well, then you're in luck, son! I haven't had the chance to put the sign up yet, but all Christmas gifts are 50% off from now until the holiday! Do you know what that means?

"Yes, Mr. Shinjo!" Midori's voice rose as he responded. "It means this is only three cents, right?"

"Right!" the old man beamed.

As he left the store, Midori placed the purple trinket, now wrapped in holiday paper by Mr. Shinjo, into his pants pocket.

There, it bumped up against Thumbprint, which Midori had taken along for the journey to town. Midori kept his hands in his pockets as he walked, partially to protect them from the cold, and partially to be certain that his precious trinket and Thumbprint both made it home safely.

A tiny glimmer of daylight remained when Midori opened the front door to his house. He first caught sight of his little sister, Setsuko, her black hair pulled back in a perfect braid. She was setting the table under mom's careful direction while Papa, Roy, Jack and KG worked near the woodstove.

"Hey, Squirt!" Jack called out. "You trying to get out of helping us? Go out back and get some firewood!"

Midori nodded and headed for the back door to the tiny home. It was no more than 15 steps from the front door to the back, and he was soon outside again. A slight shiver found its way up his spine as he paced over to the woodpile. He hoisted two solid logs and headed back towards the door. Once there, he dropped the logs so he could unlatch the door and prop it open with his foot. He then knelt, being sure to keep the toes of his left foot pressed firmly against the door and picked the logs up again before sliding back inside.

Papa, Roy, and Jack had the fire lit and flaming in no time. The chill lifted rapidly, leaving a glowing warmth in its place. After dinner, the smiling Setsuko and her big brothers began to clear the dishes.

"I miss George!" Setsuko suddenly cried out, her smile vanishing in an instant.

"Now, now, little one," Mama placed her arm over the little girl's shoulder. "We all miss George, but he's doing well in California with the cousins. Maybe we will go to visit him one day soon," she continued, her voice trailing off.

CHAPTER SEVEN

Pasadena, California

July 1927

"That box still needs to be moved, little man," George smiled.

Midori stood and grabbed the box of oranges. He lugged it to the side of the stand and dropped it. Leaning over, he took out his pocketknife and sliced open the top of the box. He pulled back the two flaps he'd created and began to remove the oranges. He placed each orange neatly on the first shelf of the stand that he'd meticulously cleaned an hour earlier.

George's produce stands were becoming well known in Pasadena for their high-quality fruit and vegetables, and their fair pricing. Midori had joined his older brother at the end of the school year a month earlier. George desperately needed help at his growing business, but Roy and Jack were working for the St. Paul and Tacoma Lumber Company, logging the Kapowsin Timberlands, and KG was too young. So, it was up to seventeen-year-old Midori to fill in as best he could.

For a month, Midori hoisted boxes and arranged produce for George. He worked tirelessly, but it never seemed to get easier. He watched as George effortlessly lifted box after box. All Midori could do was shrug and keep at it.

"Okay, Midori-san, that's all for today," George called out. "Another busy day, eh?"

Midori nodded as he closed his pocketknife and dropped it into his pants pocket. He stood watching his big brother as the young man continued to lift boxes. "Aren't we done, George?" he inquired.

"You go on ahead home, Midori. I'm just going to do a bit more to make tomorrow easier. I'll be home in 15 minutes, maybe ten. "

"No, no, no, George, I will stay too, then," Midori replied as he pulled the knife back out of the pants pocket, forcing his lips into a tiny smile.

After what felt like an eternity, George finally stopped lifting boxes. He leaned against a wall in the storeroom behind the produce stand, his face glistening. He took a deep breath, pushed himself off the wall, and headed towards his little brother. Tousling Midori's hair, George led the way out of the storeroom and into the fading sunlight.

The brothers walked quickly home. The sun was dropping lower in the sky, and the temperature was descending with it. The almost complete lack of humidity contributed to the quick-drying of what little sweat the two had produced. By the time they were ten minutes into their walk, all signs of perspiration were but a distant memory.

"Tonight I will boil some noodles to go with these vegetables,

Midori. You could use a bit of fattening up!"

Midori smiled wanly. "I can help you cook, George."

The older boy nodded and cuffed his younger brother on the shoulder. "Yes, you can little one, or you can clean up since Hede will be coming over to say hi later."

"Oh, oh, oh, are you going to take her for a walk again, George?" Midori giggled. "I know what that means, George!" Midori side stepped George's swipe at him and dodged a second playful punch.

"Okay," George called out as they stepped through the door to his one-bedroom apartment. "Go get washed up. I am going to start dinner."

Midori smiled. "George is in a hurry," he sang out. This time George didn't let Midori escape. He cornered his younger brother against the bathroom wall and grabbed him in a head-lock. Midori giggled as he tried to kick his way free. George swung his brother around a few times before dropping him gently on the floor.

"Wash up, little wise guy," George smiled.

By the time Midori made his way out of the bathroom, George had finished preparing dinner, and the two sat down to piping hot bowls of rice noodles, cabbage, carrots, and green beans.

"You feel better now that you're cleaned up, young man?" George asked.

"I feel fine," Midori replied. "How do you feel?"

"Hede is going to be here in 45 minutes, so I feel fine too!" George replied. "You sure you're okay? You seem tired, Midori."

"I told you, George, I am okay, but thank you for asking."

The two brothers ate in silence for a while. Then, George paused, holding his spoon away from his mouth. "Do you miss Seattle, Midori?" he asked.

"I miss Mama and Papa. And, I miss some of my friends, but since I changed schools two years ago, I didn't see them so much anyway."

"Tell me about that change, Midori. I know that you went to the Caucasian school, but how did that happen? Was that Mama and Papa's idea?"

"No, no, no," Midori replied quickly. "It was my idea. We are in America, George. I want to be American. I mean, I was even baptized as a Presbyterian."

"Maybe you should have been born into the Beppu family! I mean, your friend Taft and his brothers who are named Lincoln and Grant. Can't get more American than that!"

Midori arched his eyebrow at his older brother but did not answer him.

"Midori, do you not know what I'm talking about?"

"Not really. . ."

"Taft, Lincoln, and Grant were all American presidents. Too bad Mama and Papa named you 'Midori'!"

"Hey, they named you 'George'!"

George smiled. "You may be small, but you certainly are smart! I'm going to wash up before Hede gets here. You clean up, okay?"

Midori took a deep breath and stood up. He steadied himself on the back of the wooden kitchen chair. He felt lightheaded for what seemed like an eternity before it passed. He shuffled over to the sink carrying the dinner plates and placed them down. Slowly, he scrubbed the dinner remnants away and cleaned all of the utensils as well.

When he finished, Midori collapsed on the couch in the room immediately adjacent to the kitchen. It wasn't fair to call it a living room since it doubled as Midori's bedroom as well. The apartment had only one actual bedroom, and George used that. Everything would start to get tricky in a few minutes when Hede arrived. There were all sorts of rules relating to single women being in men's apartments. Midori wasn't sure if these were the landlord's rules, Japanese rules or just rules of society. What was also unclear was how much, if at all, Hede and George cared about the rules.

When Hede walked into the room a short while later, Midori

blushed and looked down at his feet. She had lustrous black hair that was brushed so smoothly behind her that it almost looked painted onto the back of her royal blue dress. She was short and even a bit squat, but she had the friendliest, most self-assured, smile Midori had ever seen.

"Hello, Midori," she smiled. "How was your day at the produce stand? Did George work you hard?"

"Um," Midori started, before stopping and glancing away. "Um, it was okay, and I'm okay. How are you, Hede, I like your dress!"

"Thank you, Midori," Hede replied behind sparkling eyes. "Thank you very much. I am fine."

At that moment, George bounded out of the bedroom. He and Hede briefly embraced before George announced, to Midori's relief, that he and Hede would be taking a walk.

As the couple left, Midori again laid down on the couch. He reached under the soft cushion and retrieved Thumbprint. Lying on his back, Midori rolled Thumbprint around in his hand, stopping every so often to count the speckles on the rock's underside.

The next thing Midori knew, George was gently waking him. "Midori-san, it's morning. Time for us to go to work." Midori stared up at his oldest brother, uncomprehending. How could it possibly be morning?

Midori frantically searched the couch with his right hand until he found Thumbprint. He exhaled and smiled as he placed the rock under the cushion. He pushed himself up, straightened his clothes, and headed for the bathroom down the hall.

The day unfolded, slowly at first, then picked up its pace. By midday, Midori was struggling to keep up. Customers seemed to be coming in waves. Each time it seemed that he had re-stocked the display shelves, the oranges, in particular, would be gone. Midori would pick himself up and head back to the cool, dark storeroom where he would hoist a box over his head and carry it back out front. Before he could even fully empty a box, customers would appear, as if from nowhere, and begin plucking oranges from underneath him.

Despite the canopy covering most of the produce, Midori and George often spent much of their time in direct sunlight. Midori always wore a walking hat to try to block the sun, and he spent considerable time dabbing his face with water from the omnipresent buckets. Still, the dry heat was unrelenting.

The heat and the physical labor, which had been chasing Midori for months, finally caught him one day in late August. As morning broke, George arose and looked down at his little brother, but the young man had nothing left to give.

"George, I am so sorry," Midori's voice quivered as he spoke. "I, I don't think I can get up."

"Little man, you don't seem well. It's okay; I will pick up someone to help me today. You stay here. You will be better tomorrow."

But, Midori was not better tomorrow. Or the day after.

It was about a month later that Mama and Papa Shimoda arrived from Seattle. As a gift upon his retirement, Papa's company gave them a fancy ocean cruise that delivered them from Seattle to Los Angeles where they would be able to once again be near their children.

Mama's initial excitement at seeing her two boys quickly gave way to concern. She pulled George aside and questioned him about Midori's health. How long had he been exhibiting these symptoms of sheer exhaustion? Why had George not written sooner?

Mama and Papa's arrival quickly changed the daily routine. Papa now went to the produce stand to help George, while Mama tended to Midori. She offered up cod liver oil and many hours lying in the sun as remedies. Some days Midori insisted he was healthy and energetic enough to join his brother and father. Others, he couldn't drag himself off of the couch.

George's small apartment couldn't hold the four Shimodas for long. Mama and Papa took over George's bedroom, and George slept on a mattress on the floor next to Midori's couch. The communal bathroom down the hall was already a hive of activity. Adding Papa caused a bit more crowding, but adding Mama was a whole new dimension. The neighbors began to grumble and accuse the Shimodas of monopolizing the bathroom. George smoothed things over by assuring them that Mama and Papa were looking for a new place to live. Still, the tension was palpable.

Midori was about to start his junior year in high school. It would be his first year of school in Pasadena and his third school in four years. After spending his junior high years in a school in Seattle that was populated heavily with Japanese Americans, Midori had transferred to a school where he was one of only a handful of non-Caucasian students. Despite his diminutive stature, Midori had continued to play basketball with the much taller white boys.

In the weeks leading up to the start of his junior year at John Muir High in Pasadena, Midori shuttled to doctor after doctor under Mama's watchful eye in an attempt to have them diagnose his ongoing fatigue. By the time school was to start, Midori felt marginally better. He hadn't worked at the produce stand for weeks; still, his energy ebbed and flowed with no apparent pattern.

As the first days of school turned to weeks, it was clear that Midori still wasn't strong enough to return to the produce stand after classes ended. He also had no energy for sports, so basketball was not an option. No one was sure what was wrong with Midori, though one doctor repeatedly referred to his malady as mononucleosis. Whatever it was, it certainly lingered.

One late October afternoon, on a day when there was just a hint of the almost non-existent Fall in the air, Midori returned from school with an idea.

"Mama, I met some boys at school today who talked to me about photography," Midori began.

"What kind of boys, Midori?" Mama asked.

Midori arched his eyebrow and scratched his cheek. "What kind of boys, Mama? What do you mean?"

"Good boys? Nice boys?"

"Oh," Midori smirked. "Yes, Mama, good boys. They only do good things," Midori smiled.

Mama pursed her lips and stared at Midori for a moment before smiling. "Okay, what kind of photography Midori-san?"

They take pictures of everything, Mama! I've seen some of them; they are beautiful."

"Oh? You mean they take pictures of girls?" Mama's eyes twinkled as she spoke.

"Mama!"

"Midori, how do you know about photography? So much to learn?"

"I don't know, Mama, I just found it interesting, so I asked a lot of questions," Midori blushed.

LEFT TO RIGHT: BIG GEORGE, ROY, SETSUKO, JACK, KG, MAMA
SHIMODA, PASADENA, C 1925

PORTRAIT TAKEN FOR CHRISTMAS POSTCARD – DECEMBER
1926

CHAPTER EIGHT

Laguna Beach, CA

February 1933

"Thank you for allowing me to come and learn from you, Mr. Mortensen," Midori said as the photographer opened his door.

"Let's see how it goes, young man. Come on in. There is a room in the basement that you can use. Follow me."

Midori carried his tightly cinched cloth with three shirts, a few pairs of underwear and socks, and followed Mortensen down the stairs. To call the room "spare" would be charitable. It contained a bed frame and nothing more.

"Sorry, there's no mattress. We can bring you to Olson's in town and see whether they have something you can put together to sleep on."

Midori ran every third or fourth step as he accompanied Mortensen out the door. The latter's opinions were as authoritative as his stride and his long legs chewed up the ground in rapid fashion.

"This is a tough time to get into the photography business, young man. Ever since the market crash, people seem only to have money to spend on food or clothes. Essentials. Pictures aren't essential to most people. The wealthy, those who haven't lost everything, they are my remaining clientele."

"As I said in my letter, my goal is to learn from you, Mr. Mortensen. I will also, of course, help your business in any way I can. I am not interested in making any money from you. Just learning."

"Very noble of you, kind sir," Mortensen smiled. "Of course, it's up to you whether you think what I have to teach is of value. That jackass, Ansel Adams, would be quick to tell you to not waste your time with me. He doesn't approve of the way I retouch photos. But, all he ever does is photograph landscapes. Where are the people? You know he thinks I'm the devil, right?"

Midori nodded slowly. "I have read a bit about his comments. I am here to learn from you, sir. I am especially keen to learn about your silver bromide technique, Mr. Mortensen."

"Well, if that's all I can teach you, then you've wasted your time. Many can teach you that. I hope to teach you why pictures of people are more interesting than pictures of landscapes. And how you can touch them up. Meantime, let's get into town and get you some stuff."

Midori bought some rope at Olson's and used it to fashion a spring base of sorts for his bed frame. Mortensen gave him some blankets, one of which he used as a pillow. Not exactly luxury, but it worked, and became Midori's home for the next few months.

Mortensen's petite wife, Courtney, left the two men alone for the better part of each day before checking in on them to discuss dinner plans. Dinners were sparse but tasty and healthful for the most part. Midori had offered to pay for his food, but the Mortensens quickly refused. To carry his weight, Midori went to town every few days and returned with a sack of fresh fruit and vegetables.

In the studio, it was all work. Mortensen had a dark room full of toys. He demonstrated to Midori how to manipulate his images to make them look more like paintings than pictures.

"Adams shoots mountains and rivers and places of natural beauty, and that's fine," Mortensen began one afternoon. "But, people, in various poses, are the most interesting, the most intriguing of all subjects. The photographs that capture the heart are the ones of people we love or people we are taken in by. What do people do when they see a beautiful scene? They have a friend or family member pose in front of it, right? Ansel, the great. Ansel, the head of the big f64 club. Why is it so personal for him? He should do his thing, and I will do mine!"

Midori soaked up the controversial photographer's every word. He learned how to bromide a photograph to make it look like a charcoal painting as well as other techniques used to soften the image and have it appear to be more painting-like. At first, Mortensen would have Midori observe during a shoot, and he'd then test Midori on what he'd seen and heard. Once Mortensen was convinced that his young protégé was fully prepared to be an apprentice, he began to allow Midori to help during photo shoots.

One particularly beautiful late Spring day, Mortensen greeted Midori with a huge smile. "Today is going to be a special day," Mortensen began.

"Why is that, Mr. Mortensen?" Midori asked.

"We have a very special photoshoot today, young man! Get the equipment and join me on the front porch. Soon you will see what I mean."

For the next thirty minutes, the two men lugged their equipment on the bus and exchanged small talk about angles, lighting, and the developing of pictures. Midori knew better than to question Mortensen on the subject of the upcoming shoot. He would know soon enough.

As they rode the bus, Mortensen started to speak, stopped for a moment, then began again. "Midori, we are about to embark upon something very Californian, but I believe you should end up in New York City one day down the road."

Midori narrowed his eyes and asked, "Why is that Mr. Mortensen?"

"The best of the best are in New York City. You have a unique gift; a rare eye. You should go to New York City, so your eye is not wasted."

The pair walked for several blocks after being dropped off by the bus. The homes were magnificent, and Midori's pulse quickened at the thought of whom they might be shooting. Eventually, they reached the front of a huge, fenced-in home, with white columns, a large, wraparound porch, and pastel blue shutters. Mortensen reached over the fence, fiddled for a moment, and produced a small key. He placed the key in the hole on the gate, and it swung open. They walked onto the property and Mortensen stopped and replaced the key and closed the gate behind them.

Midori stared, first at the opulent house, then at his mentor, but the latter's face betrayed nothing. No twinkle in the eye, no upturned lip showing a smile. Nothing.

Mortensen grabbed the large brass knocker and banged it twice against the front door. "Sometimes they don't hear it, so you have to bang," he smiled.

"Mr. Mortensen, please come in." The tall man, wearing impossibly long white gloves, nodded at Midori. "And you, sir, are?"

"I am Midori Shimoda; I am assisting Mr. Mortensen."

"Apprentice. Midori here is going to be a wonderful photographer in his own right, one day," Mortensen smiled.

"Very good, sir, please, both of you, do come in. I will let Ms. Wray know you are here."

Midori almost lost his breath at the mention of Fay Wray, one of the stars of *King Kong*, the hottest movie of the year. He turned to Mortensen and began to speak, but the photographer put his finger to his lips, motioning Midori not to ask any questions.

"William!" Fay called out, her arms outstretched in front of her in greeting.

"Fay!" called out Mortensen as he grabbed her hands and pulled her toward him. The two embraced warmly before stepping back. "This is Midori, my apprentice, Fay."

"So very pleased to meet you, Miss Wray," Midori said softly, his head tilted to the side as he averted the movie star's eyes.

"Midori," she smiled, "please, call me Fay."

Midori continued to avoid her eyes as he nodded ever so slightly. He began to unpack the equipment when Mortensen stopped him. "Not here," he said. "Fay, the pool? Or the garden, perhaps?"

"Oh, the pool sounds right for this one, William. I will head up and change and meet you gentleman out there."

Mortensen smirked as he helped Midori pack up the equipment to move to the pool area. Midori's face reddened, but he said nothing.

Once they were outside, Midori took stock of the location. He noticed the angle of the sun, the shaded areas, and the reflection off the water. "Are we doing straight portrait shots or will there be any action shots as well?" he asked.

"We will do what Fay wants, but I'm guessing it will be straight portraits, so let's set up for that."

Midori set up both tripods to the left of the pool about six feet from each other. He placed a camera in each and then walked the perimeter of the pool, glancing back toward the cameras as he walked. When he returned, Midori moved one tripod about six inches closer to the edge. He circled the pool again, this time stopping and kneeling on the other side as he faced the camera. Finally, he was satisfied.

Midori looked up just in time to see Fay entering the pool area wearing a bathing suit and a white, lace cover-up. She was barefoot, though she carried a pair of sandals in her right hand.

"I've asked Clark to bring us some lemonade, gentlemen, but we can certainly get started whenever you're ready."

With that, the photoshoot began. Mortensen knew the parameters of the shoot, but Midori was left to guess since the photographer hadn't shared anything with him. It seemed to just be some general, poolside publicity photos, which wouldn't have been too difficult, but for the fact that Fay had to interrupt every few minutes to take phone calls. Most of the calls were short and she was very apologetic, but there was absolutely no flow to the session.

"William, I so apologize," the star began as she came out from the house yet again.

Mortensen waved off any worries. "Okay, let's have you over by the left side of the pool," he began, but Midori quickly approached and whispered in his ear.

"Oh, right, Midori has reminded me that we shot those already. Let's move you here, toward the front of the pool."

Midori walked with Fay around toward the front of the pool. As the actress loosened her cover-up to show her bathing suit, Midori gently motioned to her to move a few feet to the right. He then approached her. "May I?" he asked, pointing to her cover-up.

"Yes, do what you think will help the shot," Fay smiled.

Midori pulled the cover- up back ever so slightly and cinched it together in the back. He then expertly tucked it into the back of Fay's bathing suit in a way that wasn't visible from the front. Mortensen nodded approvingly and finally took his first shot of her in the new location. After each snap of the camera, Midori quickly replaced the plate so Mortensen could take another picture, but it was a tedious affair at best.

By the time they finished with the shoot, the dinner hour had approached.

"I'm so very sorry it took so long," said Fay. "Thanks for your patience, gentlemen. I can't wait to see the pictures! I'd invite you two to stay for dinner, but I have plans to dine out with John and some friends."

"Fay, it's always a pleasure to see you and to work with you! Please tell Billy I said hello the next time you speak with him," said Mortensen. "I will get you the pictures just as soon as we can develop them."

"Ah, Billy! I think you know, William, he's the one of all my siblings who always stays in touch. Of course, since *King Kong*, I've suddenly heard from the others. Funny how that works, isn't it, William?" Fay said, with a grin that displayed not a trace of resentment.

As soon as they left the mansion, Midori turned to Mortensen. "You know her brother, then?"

"Yes," Mortensen nodded. "Billy was a good friend of mine. I mean, he still is, he's just not around, so I don't see much of him. I actually brought Fay to California, back around 1920 or so. I was in Utah visiting Billy. He asked me to escort his little sister to California. She was maybe 13 or 14 then. The family was moving to California, and they needed some help getting everyone here. I don't remember all the details, but I've known the whole family for quite some time. Her parents are Mormons. They lived in the Mormon community near Salt Lake City, but, for some reason, decided to move to Hollywood. Fay started acting while she was still in high school. She didn't give a damn for the whole religion thing. Anyway, quite fun, don't ya' think?"

Midori nodded and smiled. "Yes, I can honestly say I wasn't expecting that!"

"How could you, I never told you about Fay."

"You're full of surprises, Mr. Mortensen," Midori grinned.

"Here's another one, Midori. It's time you called me 'William.' No more 'Mr. Mortensen.'

Thank you, Mr., I mean, William!"

While we're at it, I think you should move your stuff up from the basement. We have a nice guest room, but few guests. Why don't you move in there?"

"Three wonderful things, all in one day. Thank you, William," Midori smiled.

CARNIVAL OF ONIONS, EARLY 1930S, GELATIN SILVER PRINT

CONDUCTOR, EARLY 1930S, GELATIN SILVER PRINT

CYCLONE, EARLY 1930S, GELATIN SILVER PRINT

CHAPTER NINE

Pasadena, CA

July 8, 1937

Midori hung up the phone and asked his assistant to cancel the rest of his appointments and lock up. He took his small brownie camera and headed out the door. As he walked, his mind wandered back to Japan. Try though he might, he couldn't remember when Mama had left him the first time. But, his memory of boarding the Africa Maru without her, George, Roy, or Jack was still seared in his mind. He thought of Aiko and smiled at the young woman's kindness. He wondered if she'd found happiness in America.

As he continued making his way along the narrow street, Midori pulled Thumbprint from his pocket. He pawed at the small indentation and then held the rock tightly. Finally, he took stock of his whereabouts and turned. He'd have to head over to see Papa and the rest of the family.

Mama had been sick for some time, so her death shouldn't have come as a surprise. Still, George's call had jolted Midori. When he'd seen Mama the week before, he knew that the end was near. Just how near, no one can ever really tell. At least that's what the doctor had said. So, Midori had assumed there would be more visits. More times to hold her hand. More times to say, "I love you, Mama."

Midori smiled as he remembered their final visit together. Mama had told him that she was proud of him. They laughed as they remembered the day Midori had come from school and told Mama he was interested in being a photographer. Mama complimented him on his work. Midori bit the inside of his mouth as he remembered saying, "Mama, I am proud to be your son."

CHAPTER TEN

Pasadena, CA

December 6, 1941

"Before I propose a toast, I have a few words to offer." The speaker was Floyd Evans, Midori's closest friend over the last decade. Floyd looked out at the thirty or so friends sitting and standing in the comfortable, though now quite crowded, living room of the house Midori shared with his father and his sister.

"My man, Midori, here," Floyd began as he swept his arm in Midori's direction, "as you all know, doesn't boast about his accomplishments. So, tonight, it's up to me to do that for him!

We are gathered here to celebrate Midori completing his 500th professional photoshoot since opening his own studio in 1934. This is truly an amazing feat given the terrible condition of our economy, and how little some people have to spend on things like pictures. It's a testament to Midori that he's succeeded so fantastically and he's barely over thirty years old.

"But, you see, Midori isn't just a great photographer. He's a smart businessman too. His clients have included California Institute of Technology, University of Southern California, Pasadena Junior College where he also teaches aspiring photographers, and Whittier and Pomona Colleges. He knew they wouldn't run out of money and would always need yearbooks. And, he cultivated a perfect clientele, relocated Easterners of means who recognize his talent. They seem to still have money, too, just like the colleges. So, Midori has made quite a business for himself. And, Midori probably knows more about Pasadena society than any gossiper there is!"

"Okay, that's enough, Floyd," Midori smiled as he scrambled to stand next to his much taller friend. "Thank you for the kind words about my business. As for the last comment, well, I do what's necessary for business."

Floyd draped his right arm around Midori. With his left arm, he raised his glass. "To my wonderful and devoted friend, Midori. May we celebrate again when you hit 1000, and then again at each additional thousand. Truly, my friend, nothing can stop you now!"

The friends cheered as Floyd finished his toast. Midori then stood. "Floyd, you are a wonderful friend. Thank you. I always know I can count on you. You have introduced me to all of the wonderful members of the community I work with. My business would be nowhere without you. And, best of all, you never expect anything in return. You are the definition of a true friend."

"Yes, Midori, you know you can always count on me. But not just me. Gordon, Tom and Helen will always be there for you, too, not to mention all the others here tonight."

At that, Midori's oldest brother, George, clambered to his feet. "Midori," he began, "Floyd is too nice, you know that, right?" He continued as Midori smiled and nodded. "You're still the little one in the family, no matter how successful you become! Okay, seriously. Roy, Jack, KG, Setsuko, we're all proud of you. And, of course, Papa, too. I have watched you grow up and become successful, little man. You are smart and you work hard. You have chosen wisely to become a photographer and to choose colleges and wealthy people as clients. Midori, Floyd is right. Nothing can stop you now!"

George raised his glass and turned to his brother. "To the best darn photographer in California! Aw, heck, make that the entire West Coast! Floyd, we will leave it up to you. Stay on Midori and count up his clients. When he approaches 1000, let's start to plan the next celebration. To my brother, Midori! Nothing can stop him now!"

RAKE, GELATIN SILVER PRINT, 1930S

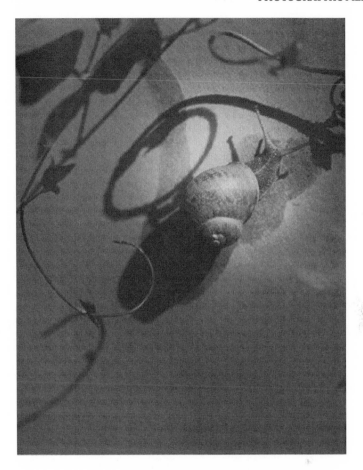

SNAIL, GELATIN SILVER PRINT, MID-1930S

SETSUKO, GELATIN SILVER PRINT, MID-1930S

YAMATO, GELATIN SILVER PRINT, MID-1930S

STAFF PHOTO, 1942 POMONA COLLEGE METATE

PART TWO

CHAPTER ELEVEN

Pasadena, CA

March 1, 1942

Midori sat at the kitchen table in the family home and tried to focus on the newspaper. *The Examiner* had one of its typical screaming headlines, "FDR to Japs: Get Out of the West Coast or Else!" On February 19th, President Roosevelt had issued an executive order requiring that all people of Japanese descent leave the West Coast or be subject to incarceration in "camps." Rumors were rampant that the military would soon be knocking down the doors of all Japanese—American citizens or resident aliens-- and taking them into custody.

"Okay, Sets," Midori said to his sister, as he looked up from the paper, "the plan is set. We leave right around dusk and drive through the night. I don't know how far we will get. Floyd will fill the tank with gas, so we can go for a while. How is May?"

"She's nervous, like all of us, Midori. Do you think this is the best plan?"

"I do, Sets," Midori began before stopping and looking at his sister more closely. "You are always dressed so beautifully. I hope you will be comfortable on the long drive."

When his sister didn't reply, Midori continued, "It's also the only plan. What else can we do? We can't stay. The order from the President says all Japanese-all aliens and non-aliens, he said - must be relocated away from California. Away from the whole West Coast. We've both heard the rumors. We will be arrested and sent to those camps if we don't leave. It's not worth going over again, I'm sorry."

"Okay, so George, Hede, and the girls are going with Papa and Roy and his family to Utah as well, right?

Midori smiled. "George, Hede, and the girls are going with Papa, yes. Remember, they are taking Hede's brother, Louie's employee, and his two brothers as well, which is why they don't have room for May. Roy, who knows? He is so nonchalant he either doesn't think anything will happen or he doesn't realize that he has to hustle to avoid being sent to a camp. But, the others are going to a place called Mapleton or Springville, maybe. Hede gave me a post office box that we can write to."

"Lucky for Jack and KG that they are far away and don't need to deal with this," Setsuko replied.

"Lucky, indeed. If they are smart, they will not return. Not even try."

"Who are these people, our sponsors, again?" Setsuko sniffed.

"You know how I work on some college yearbooks, right? Well, Billy Jones is the student staffer for one of them. When he heard about the Evacuation Order, he offered to have us go to his parents' farm in Monticello, Utah. They've decided to raise turkeys and need help on the farm. Billy says they are 100% supportive of us coming to live there and have us help with the farm."

Setsuko smiled. "I understand," she smirked. "Because we are such fine farmers!"

As Setsuko turned on her high heels and headed back towards the bedroom, Midori laughingly continued: "Anyway, the tank is 18 gallons. If we are lucky, we can get 250 miles, maybe a few more, before we need to refuel. By my calculation, we will be in the desert then. I've driven that way before, but I can't say I remember where the gas stations are."

"Or if they will let us refuel," Setsuko sighed. "Are we really going to a farm? This is crazy."

"Right, if they will let us refuel," Midori nodded, again ignoring the second part of his sister's remarks. "Do you need any help getting May ready?"

Setsuko shook her head, turned and sashayed away.

Dusk approached rapidly, and the temperature dropped as quickly as the sun. Midori shivered involuntarily as he lifted his mother's fully loaded silver chest into the trunk of his burgundy Chevy Coupe. Beyond that, each of the three occupants of the car took one suitcase and a small bag. Midori arranged and re-arranged the suitcases until everything fit just right.

Having said their goodbyes over the past few days, Midori, his overly dressed, heavily made-up sister, Setsuko, and their brother George's seven-year-old daughter, May, climbed into the car and drove east without looking back.

Midori tuned -in radio station KFI as the three began their journey.

"Well, everyone, this is Jimmy Johnson, coming to you on KFI in LA! It certainly was reassuring to hear President Roosevelt's Fireside Chat last week, wasn't it? It seems like after we took it on the chin at Pearl Harbor, we've righted things pretty quickly. I've got to admit it, though. I'm glad the President asked us to have a world map in front of us for the chat! He spoke about places I've never heard of, that's for sure. But, if the Japs and Krauts think they can go there and hide from us and the Brits, well, they've got another thing coming to them."

The radio was remarkably clear as Midori let out the clutch and headed down the quiet road. The streets were far less lively now that the country was at war. Apparently, having fun had been outlawed. The patrons in the few neon-signed establishments that remained open shared a steely reserve. Jaws looked tighter, and the drinking was more purposeful.

The disc jockey continued, "you know, I was never one of those who got caught up in politics before this darn war. I never even heard of the "Yellow Peril" before Pearl Harbor, and I'd probably not have believed you if you told me about it last year. But, I've been reading a lot about it in the *Examiner* these past few weeks and you know what, folks? William Randolph Hearst was not nuts! No, sirree, he was, it turns out, completely correct to warn us about the Japs."

Midori rolled through town, careful to stay within the speed limit, but equally as careful to not go so slowly as to draw notice. Before long, the trio had cleared the Pasadena city limits, and darkness enveloped them. Seven-year-old May was soon asleep, her long black hair covering the better part of her face. Setsuko was starting to nod off as well. KFI kept Midori company for a while, but it, too, soon faded, leaving Midori alone with his thoughts.

The day after one of the best days in Midori's life had dawned sunny and mild. With Christmas rapidly approaching, Midori had three shoots on December 7, 1941, so he got up early and began his ritual preparation. He cleaned lenses, prepped the developing trays, swept the studio clean, and made sure everything in sight was spotless. Two of the shoots were to be at the studio and one on-site at a high school. A somewhat early, holiday season play was taking place at an exclusive girls' school and Midori had been hired by several of the parents to photograph their daughters both as they prepped for the show and during the show itself.

Late that morning, in the middle of the second studio shoot, one of Midori's assistants had interrupted him. Hana had never interrupted Midori before. He still winced at the thought of how he'd reacted. "Hana, hold your tongue, please," he'd said. "But, sir, please, it's very important," she'd replied.

Midori sighed as he remembered that morning. Somehow, they'd finished the shoot, but the school sessions were canceled. Everything was canceled. Midori had headed to the house he temporarily shared with his father and his sister, where the family had gathered. As they came to grips with the fact that the unthinkable had happened, the family pondered its fate.

Midori pursed his lips as he remembered George warning everyone that all Japanese, whether American citizens or not, were going to have a rough time. "We will not be welcome any longer," Midori remembered George saying. As usual, Midori's big brother had proved prophetic.

In the immediate aftermath of the bombing of Pearl Harbor, Midori saw a rather steep drop in business. Some now former clients were transparent in their belief that Midori was no better than an enemy combatant. Others made up little stories. They were going to call off the shoot entirely, they'd say, because of the war. Only Midori would learn through the small photography community that they had scheduled with one of his competitors. One of his Caucasian American competitors.

Midori slowed as he began to enter the Angeles National Forest. There were no streetlights, the forest itself was dense, and the roads were, at best, intermittently paved. Midori yawned once and then a second time. Despite the cool, late Winter air, Midori rolled down the window. The breeze immediately made its presence felt, and Midori found himself becoming more alert. Setsuko began to stir. She pulled her lightweight, silk jacket tighter as her eyes fluttered open. She glanced over toward Midori and started to laugh.

"Did you have a funny dream, sister, or is it me who is the object of your laughter?" Midori inquired.

"I'm sorry, Midori, but you look funny in that driving suit," Setsuko giggled again.

Midori allowed himself a tight grin. "It keeps me warm, Sets, so you and May can sleep, and I can open the windows to keep me awake. And, I may look funny in it, but you are the one who will freeze in that dress of yours!"

"Where are we?"

"We're in the Angeles National Forest. Floyd and I have driven through here before on our way to the Mojave. I'm pretty sure we're still east of San Bernardino. I know there's a road that will head left and take us north through the forest and up towards Barstow. The goal is Baker by daybreak, and then we'll need a place to lay low until dark."

"Midori, do you think they are going to round up every Japanese person on the entire West Coast? I think I remember hearing that there are over 100,000 of us. Can't we try to find a motel, at least? They can't catch 100,000 people all at once."

"You say, 'us,' but remember, I do not have American citizenship. George, Roy, Jack, KG, they all do. So do you, even if you have a Japanese name like me. The authorities," and here Midori swept his left arm off the steering wheel and made a large circle with it, "think of me as a foreigner, sympathetic to the enemies of America. Like I said when we were leaving, I can't leave my situation to chance. We've been told to leave the West Coast, and we need to follow that order. No motels, sorry."

Suddenly, Midori slowed and veered to his right into a small opening in the trees. He turned off the motor and the lights and placed his fingers on his lips, warning Setsuko to be quiet. Setsuko glanced over her shoulder, first at her niece, who remained asleep, then into the distance, where she saw the faintest hint of the headlights that had spooked Midori. She shook her head and slumped down. Midori, too, slouched in his seat.

As the car approached, Midori could hear May rustling in the tiny back seat. "Uncle Midori," she said, sleep still very much evident in her voice, "what's going on, where are we?"

"May, please pretend to be asleep until the car behind us passes, then I will answer," came Midori's clipped reply.

Midori slumped still further into his seat as the car now inched past. Midori's hands were stuffed in his pockets, the left one of which held his wallet, and the right one of which held his beloved Thumbprint, the rock that had gotten him through worse situations than this. As the taillights began to fade in the distance, Midori let out a small sigh and assured May that they'd be on their way soon. The three sat up in their seats, and Midori turned the key in the ignition switch. Just as the engine jumped to life, Midori turned it off and motioned to the others to slump down again. Headlights were approaching again, this time from in front of them.

"Do you think we should move the car so it's less visible, Midori?" Setsuko asked.

"No, we need to leave it in the same spot. If that's the same car that just passed us and it's now coming back, I want them to think we're sleeping, so they don't stop. If we move the car, they may notice."

"What if they stop because they think we've broken down?"

"Anyone who was broken down here at this hour would get out and wave for help, Sets. Let's lay low and hope it works."

The car approached and slowed. Midori fought the urge to sit up straight in his seat to see what was going on. He clutched Thumbprint tightly and held his breath. The engine kept chugging. Soon the car was past, and Midori pulled himself up partway in his seat so he could look out the rearview mirror. He saw the taillights and began to exhale. But, the lights seemed to no longer be moving.

"Darn, I think the car is backing up, Sets," Midori said through a clenched jaw. He took a deep breath and then continued, in a much lighter tone, "wait, I think it's now stopped backing up. It's turning! This is wonderful news! I bet we missed the turn back there where they're turning. They missed it too and turned around to go back to it."

Midori turned the key in the ignition, and the Coupe came to life. May was nodding off to sleep again, but Setsuko picked herself up and smiled. "Looks like we are lucky, tonight, brother!"

Midori edged the car back down the impossibly dark path that passed for a road until he saw the opening on his right. Without the inadvertent help from the other motorist there was no way he'd have located this road. They likely would have driven miles off course.

Midori inched the car forward, scanning the bushes on either side for any sign of an ambush. After he'd driven a few hundred yards, Midori gently pushed on the gas pedal and the car picked up speed. The trio headed north, the end of the forest their next goal.

The forest was so dense that starlight and moonlight were both unable to penetrate it. But, before long, Midori began to sense a change. The forest was thinning, and he occasionally could see ten or fifteen feet to the side of the car. There were still oak woodland trees and assorted shrubs, to be certain, but fewer of them. May and Setsuko were both sound asleep now as it was past midnight. Other than the one car, Midori hadn't seen any sign of life through the forest.

In less than an hour, Midori exited the forest and continued northeast toward Bartow. The starlit sky provided a beautiful contrast to the hours in the woods. Midori tapped his hand lightly on the steering wheel and smiled as he recognized landmarks from previous trips to the desert. He knew from experience that it was unlikely to be fruitful, but Midori nevertheless turned on the radio and tried to tune in a station. Although the static was intense and he didn't want to wake May and Setsuko, Midori was able to find KPRO at 1440 on the radio dial.

Straining to make out the banter behind the static, Midori eventually recognized it as "Abie's Irish Rose," the new weekly comedy series. Midori had only listened to one or two previous episodes, which he hadn't particularly liked, but he was in need of a diversion to keep him awake. The show must have been taped Midori thought as it was way too late to be on live.

The signal on KPRO was reasonably strong, but still faded in and out, depending upon the foliage in the area. Midori fiddled incessantly with the dial, trying to improve the sound, to no avail.

Midori suddenly realized that he needed to pee. Badly. He slowed the car, pulled over to the side and hopped out. Not having seen another vehicle for the better part of 30 minutes, Midori unzipped, stepped close to the car so as not to be seen, and relieved himself. He took a few minutes to walk around the car, stretching his arms and swaying from side to side. Eventually, he opened the door, reached into the back and pulled out an apple and an orange. He peeled the orange placing the pieces of rind in a napkin and placing it on the back floor a foot or so from May's tiny feet. He climbed back into the car and began heading toward Barstow, which he knew couldn't be far at this point.

Glancing at his watch, Midori grimaced ever so slightly. Even with the dashboard lights, he couldn't make out the time. And so, he drove on.

Lights began to appear in the distance. Not a lot of lights, but lights nonetheless. Barstow. Sixty miles from Baker, which was the final destination for the night.

Perhaps it was the lights or just the passage of time, but Setsuko stirred and awoke, followed shortly after that by May.

"Where are we, Uncle Midori?" asked May, her voice betraying the fact that she'd just awoken.

"We are passing through a town called Barstow. Nice little town where Floyd and I have stopped on trips to the desert. There's a fun ice cream shop there, but it's closed now since it's the middle of the night," Midori chuckled.

"How are you feeling, Midori?" Setsuko asked.

"Okay, I got out for a bit and stretched maybe an hour or so ago. We should be in Baker in, maybe an hour and a half."

"How are we doing on gas?"

"We will make it to Baker, but not much beyond. Under half a tank."

"Do you think anyone will let us fill up?"

"We will get gas, I promise."

It was just after 4:00 AM when Midori saw the first sign for Baker. Having spent many days in Death Valley and the Mojave Desert on picture taking forays, Midori knew Baker well, and his tense body began to relax a bit at the first sighting.

"Okay, ladies, Baker is a town I know pretty well. Just to the east is the Mojave Desert. And, back a bit and also a bit north is Death Valley. Floyd and I have been here many times, and I've been here other times too. The desert scenery has always been my favorite to photograph.

"Sets, you remember Mr. Mortensen?"

"Of course!"

"Oh, my, he didn't like the desert! Called it 'Ansel Adams territory.' He and Adams are sworn enemies. Mortensen would always say to me, "Midori, take pictures of people, not scenery. Adams takes pictures of scenery because he can't figure out what to do with people.

"Okay, there is a small park with lots of woods behind it where Floyd and I sometimes would sit and eat ice cream after lunch before heading on. Let me see if I can find it. It might be a good place to hide out for the day."

"Uncle Midori," came May's voice. "Why are we hiding? Is someone going to hurt us? Did we do something wrong?" she continued her voice rising in pitch as her fear increased.

"We did nothing wrong," Setsuko quickly replied in a soothing voice. "But, there are some people who are mad at all the Japanese people. Every one of us. Because of something other Japanese people have done. They blame us for something others have done. Do you understand that at all, May?"

"Maybe a little..."

"Okay," Midori chimed in. "Let's say your Japanese friend, Fanny, put her book bag in front of your Caucasian friend, Susie, and Susie tripped over it. Then, a week later, you were playing with Susie, and someone said to Susie, 'don't play with her; she'll trip you with her book bag."

"But, I didn't trip her, Fanny did!" May called out.

"Exactly," Midori smiled. "Exactly."

Midori found his way to the park. May got out and begged to play. Midori and Setsuko conferred before reluctantly deciding to allow their young niece some much needed time to do what little ones need to do.

Midori held the flashlight so May could see the swing. Setsuko helped her up before taking the flashlight so Midori could push. The three soaked in the peace and solitude until the eastern sky was awash in pink, signaling the start of a new day.

Having done a bit of scouting while the girls took advantage of the restrooms near the baseball field, Midori directed the car down a trail not meant for vehicles. The branches scraped and scratched the side of Midori's car, and he tried to shrug off the resulting damage by reminding himself it was the only way to enhance their chances of safety.

Once the car was fully out of sight, the three took turns sleeping. The sound of children playing in the park, a few hundred yards and a lifetime away, provided a stark reminder of their circumstances. Daylight hours, once so welcome, were now suddenly both fraught with danger and numbingly dull. Happily, the temperature was warming to a nearly perfect 70 degrees from the chill of the pre-dawn hours.

After what seemed like an eternity, the sun began to fade, and the temperature dropped noticeably. It was time to come out of hiding. And, time to try to buy gas.

"Okay," Midori said as he pulled the Coupe onto the roadway behind the park, "here's the plan. I will drive us to a block or two away from the gas station. You will then take over the wheel. I will put on my sunglasses and pretend to be blind. No one should find me intimidating at that point."

Setsuko convulsed more than a bit, a full-throated, guttural sound emanating from her tiny mouth. "Brother, what are you five one and one hundred pounds? No one could find you intimidating!"

Midori ignored his sister. "May," he said to his niece in the back seat. We are going to have to play a game of pretend, okay?"

"Okay," May replied, "can I play too?"

"Yes, but you have to play the way I tell you, okay? Otherwise, it could be a dangerous game because there are some bad people."

"What do I need to do?"

"May, you need to be very still and pretend to be sleeping while Aunt Sets buys gas for us, okay?"

May frowned. "That's all I get to do? That's not much of a game for me!"

The desert town of Baker was coming to life as Setsuko steered the Coupe into the Richfield station. Midori sat next to her with his sunglasses on as the attendant finished pumping gas for the Ford in front of them. Setsuko inched forward when the sedan pulled out. The attendant stared at her, seemingly unsure if he was allowed to ogle a Japanese woman.

"Can you please fill up the tank, sir?" she requested her eyelashes fluttering and her red lipstick causing her smile to be even more pronounced than usual.

Continuing to stare, the attendant thumbed his finger at Midori.

"What's his story?"

"That's my brother, he's blind," Setsuko explained as she continued to smile.

"Someone shoot his eyes out after you people bombed us?"

"He was born blind, sir," Setsuko replied sweetly.

"We're gonna blow Japan right off the face of the earth, lady!"

"Well," Setsuko began, "no one would say that they didn't have it coming to them."

The attendant continued to glare at Midori, but eventually relented and pumped the gas. Setsuko stepped out of the car and steadied herself on heels that were way too high. She briefly went into the small shop that housed the cash register and held a few less than appetizing snacks. She returned to the car when the attendant called out to her.

"Hey, lady, you know why we don't have much gas to sell? The Japs blew up our tankers last week near Santa Barbara. I don't care what you look like you got some nerve coming in here, lady. Now get the hell out of here before I blow up your car as payback! Go, get out!!"

Shaking, Setsuko jumped into the car. She could hear May whimpering as she pulled away.

"What was he talking about, Midori?" Setsuko asked through

RISA SHIMODA AND BOB FLESHNER

her tears.

"I, I'm not sure. We will have to try to find out. Sets. You did an amazing job there. I am so very, very proud of you! May, are you okay back there? You pretended to sleep beautifully!"

After a few short miles, Midori took back the wheel. He headed straight for Las Vegas, which he knew would have the most lights of any city east of New York. "Ah, New York." Midori sighed. Mortensen had set Midori on a course for New York, but the old master had no way of knowing a war would intervene. It was but a dream now. But, Midori knew that he needed to stay the course. To seek Shinjitsu. His own, personal Shinjitsu. *His* truth.

The drive was quiet and tedious. Despite their underlying fear, the trio found it challenging to stay alert. Setsuko and May nodded between all-out sleep and that midway point of being awake, but not functioning. Midori let his mind drift. He wondered where the rest of the family was. Were they in Utah yet, having left a few hours earlier? He knew that they'd all be okay with George and Hede in charge. What about Roy, though? And his family? Midori took a deep breath and exhaled slowly. It was going to be a long night.

It was well past midnight when Midori pointed the car up US route 91 and headed through Las Vegas. On a whim, he stopped in a gas station just north of The Pair-O-Dice casino.

"What are you doing, Midori?" Setsuko asked, concern evident in her voice. "If anything, we should have stopped at the casino," she said. "That might have been some fun."

"We're in Las Vegas. They allow gambling and prostitution; I feel like they may be less bothered by us than people in other places. I'm going to try to get some gas and snacks."

"You here to cause trouble?" the greasy attendant asked through narrowing eyes.

"No, sir, heading to Utah, just driving through. May we fill up, please?"

"Yeah, sure," he replied, wiping his hands on the bottom of his shirttail that was billowing out from his pants. 'You know what? I'm not sure if I believe you, and you didn't ask me, but here's some advice. Don't go to the casino--lots of drunks in there. People are still pretty damn pissed off at you Japs. You might not make it out of there."

"I assure you that I am heading to Utah. We have a family waiting for us. But, I do thank you for the advice and concern."

"Not concerned, pal. I don't care if you do get the crap beat out of you. Probably serve you right for Pearl Harbor and for bombing those barges."

"Sir, someone else mentioned the gas barges, but we don't know about that. What happened? If you don't mind telling me."

"Hey, you a damn spy? Are you messing with me? Whaddya mean you don't know what happened?" It's been all over the news? Can't you read? You damn people blew up our gas tankers near Santa Barbara. You keep attacking us we're gonna wipe you off the earth. Now, pay me and get the hell out of here!"

Midori quickly pulled out of the Richland station and headed northeast on 91. With a tank full of gas and a head full of quandary, he pushed on in silence. The Utah border was no more than a hundred miles away. It was the next landmark, followed quickly by St. George. Midori calculated they'd need gas twice more. Two more chances for trouble.

Before long, Setsuko and May were again lulled to sleep. Midori drove on through the endless night, alternately searching for star formations and fiddling with the radio, though the latter had offered scant diversion since Las Vegas. Midori smiled when he saw the "Welcome to Utah" sign. The Jones family's willingness to take in Midori, Setsuko, and May was heartening and gave Midori hope that maybe, just maybe, all Utahans would be equally as welcoming.

Ah, the darn Grand Canyon. Midori had thought about heading to Monticello via the southern route but feared the crowds that might be near the Grand Canyon, even in March in a wartime setting. So, he'd opted for the northern route. But, it was a barren stretch of land. Miles upon miles of nothing but scrawny bushes and dust.

Remembering a past trip with Floyd during which he'd taken some of his favorite pictures, Midori headed toward Route 9 and Zion National Park. Mortensen had not been happy with him when Midori shared with him that he'd gone to Zion and found it to be beautiful. Mortensen railed again about it being an "Ansel Adams photo op" and admonished Midori to stick to shooting people as opposed to ancient rock formations. But, tonight, Midori was thankful he'd been to Zion on more than one previous occasion. Things happen for a reason, Midori thought, as he gazed through the windshield at the brilliant moonlit sky. No such thing as coincidence.

Midori needed to stretch and pee. The tiny town of Springdale was just up the road a few miles, with Zion National Park looming on either side of it. Midori knew the Park would be closed. He was going to have to keep his eyes peeled for a different spot at which to pull over. Eventually, he saw a dirt path heading toward what appeared to be a landfill or dump, based on the signage. He slowed considerably and steered the Coupe toward the quiet of the secluded area.

Midori relieved himself by the side of the dirt path. He couldn't remember the last time he'd sensed such silence. He fingered Thumbprint and smiled. Taking his hands from his pockets, he rubbed them together as he began to realize just how cold it was. Noticing his breath as he exhaled, Midori realized that May and Setsuko would quickly get cold. As he opened the door to climb back in the Coupe, he stiffened. A car was approaching from the direction of the dump, and it was moving way too fast.

Slipping behind the wheel, Midori turned the ignition key. Without turning on his lights, he eased his foot onto the gas pedal and steered the Coupe closer to the brush on the side of the dirt path. Seconds later, a pickup truck barreled past kicking up dust in its wake. Midori exhaled as Setsuko awoke.

"Where are we, brother?" she inquired her voice coated with sleep. "And what just happened?"

"We're in a small town called Springdale in Utah. I was just taking a break by the side of a dirt road when a pickup truck came barreling past. Probably some guy with some other guy's wife,"

Midori chuckled. "Who else would it be coming from this darkness at nearly 2:00 AM?"

Midori gently backed up to clear the brush and then slid the car into gear and headed back toward the road.

"Next stop Panguitch, about 75 miles away. We'll be taking 89 north and skirting the Dixie National Forest. That's a place I've not been, but, based on the maps and what I heard from my friend Danny who's been there, we should be able to slip into the forest easily and hide during the day. Maybe we can even take a hike through there. It would be nice to get some exercise, and I bet May would like to move around a bit too.

"We will need to figure out gas again. I want to limit the stops so we won't get any in Panguitch. There are a few small towns on 89 as we head north. Probably our best bet."

"I think we should go back to pretending you are blind, brother," Setsuko offered. "That seemed to evoke at least a bit of sympathy."

"Why, because we didn't sense straight out hatred?" Midori laughed. "I'm okay with it, as long as May doesn't give us away. No quicker way for us to get in real trouble than if that happens."

"What did you say about me, Uncle Midori?" May piped up from the back seat.

"Hello, little one," Midori replied, affection evident in his voice. "May, we think that we might need to play our little game again where I pretend to be blind, and you pretend to be asleep. Would that be okay if we did that a little later?"

"Do we need to get gas again, Uncle Midori?"

"Not yet, but we will need to at least once more before we get to the Jones' farm. Maybe twice more, hard to say."

"The gas station people are mean, Uncle Midori!"

"It's like I told you yesterday, May, they think we are someone we are not. That's why we sometimes need to pretend."

"Why don't we just tell them we aren't who they think we are?" May asked with wonderful innocence.

"Ah, child, if only it were that easy. If only."

The trio spent a peaceful day in the Dixie National Forest. The air was crisp, and Midori took many deep, cleansing breaths. May ran with abandon down the trails. Her adult companions fought the urge to stifle her enthusiasm, and they let her run. The Forest was tranquil and devoid of other humans.

As daylight faded, Setsuko pulled out the bag of food that she'd packed before they left Pasadena. The cold weather had kept all of the food reasonably fresh, and the trio dined on pickles, cheese, crackers, and fruit. They drank water from a cool forest stream and refilled their canteens. The delightful interlude came to an end as they clambered back into the Coupe and headed through Panguitch and north on 89, Midori eyeing the gas tank, which now registered just under half.

Midori knew that driving at night was going to cause them to see far fewer cars, but he was still taken aback by just how isolated he felt as he drove north on 89. The Forest loomed large and ominous to the west. To the east were a few homes dotting the landscape, otherwise miles upon miles of dusty brush. Midori tried to not think about what would happen if his car broke down. Every time the thought crossed his mind, he banished it.

The engine whirred, and Midori became lost in his mind. He had tried to not think about what awaited them in Monticello, but they were now probably only a day or two away, so it was hard not to imagine what lay ahead. He had always assumed they'd be the only people of Japanese descent in Monticello, but now he began to wonder. Over 100,000 Japanese had to evacuate the West Coast. Where would they go? Maybe some others would take advantage of the "voluntary evacuation" to find a home for the time being, at least, just like Midori, Setsuko, and May.

Midori snapped out of his reverie as they approached the small town of Salina. He was sure he saw a few lights. Glancing at his watch, he saw that it was almost 9:00 PM.

"Sets, there's a gas station ahead, and it looks open. Let's do the blind man routine, quickly."

Midori pulled off the side of the road, and he and Setsuko changed places. Setsuko drove directly to the station just as the lights went out. An attendant came out and started to speak before stopping in his tracks.

"We're just about to close," said the attendant, "I, I guess I could pump you some gas."

He was a young boy, no more than 15 or 16--Native American by all appearances.

"Where're you folks heading?" he asked.

"Monticello is our final destination. Price before that," Setsuko replied.

"Be careful out there. People are pretty fired up about you guys. I mean they aren't exactly kind to me 'cause I don't look like them, but at least my people didn't bomb Pearl Harbor," he smiled.

"Well, yes, we understand, people hate the Japanese. But, you know what," Setsuko said, "we are American. We live in Pasadena. Our heritage is Japanese, but our allegiance is to America."

"Um, good luck explaining that to the country boys out this way! They'll be pushing you with a cattle prod while you talk to them about your undying allegiance to the USA. It sounds like the makings of a movie or something.

"Anyway, we got clean restrooms and some food inside. Might want to stock up before heading out again. Hey, fella, what's up, are you blind?"

Midori nodded. "Thank you for your kindness. Who are your people that you talked about?"

"I'm Indian. From the reservations just north and east of here. I'm from the Navajo tribe. My family lives on the reservation, but I live with a friend down here. Couldn't take it up there. And I hated school. I'm River, by the way. Nice to meet you folks, and, good luck. I hope I don't read about you," he chuckled.

Midori re-took the wheel a few miles after the gas station. "What a nice young man, don't you think, Sets?"

"I think he's felt some of the same hatred we have, so he treats us better. Yes, a very nice young man."

The mood in the car was decidedly brighter as they cruised north on Route 89 and then east on Route 6. Daylight was approaching from the eastern sky when they saw the sign indicating that they were entering the town of Helper.

"Feels like we should be able to stop in a town called 'Helper,' right Sets?"

"Hah, yes, but we can probably keep going a bit further, can't we?" she asked as she tugged on the hem of her dress.

"Price is a short distance. We will need to find somewhere to spend the day."

It was unusually frigid as the trio reached Price. Staying in the car all day would be tough, but Midori knew that it was too risky to venture out into town. He found a small wooded area and slowly drove the car into some brush.

"You're getting quite good at hiding the Coupe," Setsuko smiled.

"Lots of scratches on the paint now, though," Midori replied. "That makes me unhappy."

"I'm hungry!" May cried out.

"Okay, May, we will get some breakfast food out soon, I promise."

"How about a nice hot shower, Midori?" Setsuko teased.

"Ah, that would be nice, wouldn't it? Well, maybe just another day or two. We should be in Monticello by tomorrow."

"How will they greet us, Midori?" Setsuko asked, her voice expressing a seriousness that was unusual for her.

"My friend, Billy's family will be wonderful, I'm sure. They offered for us to come and stay with them, and they need our help on the turkey farm, so how could it be otherwise?"

Setsuko shook her head. "These are strange times, brother. Strange times."

The trio passed the day uneventfully. They alternately walked through the woods and napped in the car. It was a stifling existence, but none of them complained.

As yet another day of sunshine came to an end, Midori pulled out the maps. "About 190 miles to Monticello!" he cried, excitement evident in his voice. Straight down Route 191. Looks like lots more nothing for many miles, to be honest.

"We're probably going to have to wait for a while along a roadside again. I don't think we want to pull up at the Jones' house in the middle of the night."

"No? "Setsuko smiled. "You think that might not be a good idea?"

Midori noticed yet again how rapidly the sun seemed to set once it made up its mind. No lingering in the western sky after dusk. And, the warmth from the day fled just as quickly, replaced by a chill that caused Midori's muscles to tighten.

Midori pulled the car into Monticello just after 2:00 AM. There was a gas station, a post office, a courthouse and no more than a few homes. On the outskirts of what passed for downtown were a number of wheat and livestock farms. Midori knew that their sponsors, Billy's parents, lived on one of these farms raising turkeys. Daybreak would reveal which one.

Midori pulled the car over near a stand of scraggly trees. He knew he'd need to find someplace more protective, but nothing he'd passed on the way into the town held much promise. After a short break, Midori turned the ignition key and slowly directed the Coupe along the main street of Monticello. They were the only ones making a sound.

A few miles south of town, Midori spotted a dirt road to his right. He turned the wheel and navigated around some rocks until the way was clear. He drove a few hundred feet until he came upon a small barn. He scanned the area for the farmhouse he suspected must be nearby. This area was too exposed, so he drove on.

An hour later, Midori stumbled upon a sign that read, "Vanadium Corporation of America." He turned down the rutted dirt road behind the sign, but a few hundred feet farther he came upon a chain-link fence with a much larger sign that read "Private Property, No Trespassing." He clenched his teeth and swung the Coupe back around. With no more than a gallon or two of gas left in the tank, Midori knew he couldn't afford to spend the next few hours driving around endlessly looking for a refuge. He shook his head. No place to hide in this town, he thought.

Sensing he had no other choice, Midori pulled the Coupe into the lone gas station in town. He drove around the back and parked. A few interminable hours later, as the sun became reacquainted with the eastern sky, Midori knew he'd have to move the Coupe. The sign designating shop hours indicated an opening time of 8:00 AM, but Midori didn't trust that they would be safe until then. It was daylight. He needed a plan.

"Sets, I'm going to drive a very short distance back from where we came. We can pull over on the road there. If anyone comes by, I can pretend to be reading the map. Let's wait there until 8:00 and then come back to the gas station to fill up and ask if they know where the Jones' farm is."

"Well, brother, that sounds about as good as any other plan we might come up with," Setsuko smiled.

"I'm hungry!" came May's refrain from the backseat.

"Good morning, May," Setsuko replied, "you certainly have a healthy appetite!" Setsuko reached behind her for the sack of food. "Here you go, child. You don't need me to find you something. Take what you like."

An hour later, Midori guided the Coupe back into town. He drove confidently into the gas station. The attendant headed out and then stopped short as he approached the car. "Who are you, and what do you want here?" he demanded.

"Hello, sir, my name is Midori Shimoda. I am a good friend of Billy Jones, do you know him? I am looking for his parents' farm. Frederick and Ency are expecting us," the words tumbled out of Midori's mouth.

The attendant narrowed his eyes. "Billy sent you here? How do you know Billy? Is he okay?"

"Oh, yes, he's fine. He works in Los Angeles. I used to do some work with Billy. We are following the President's order to evacuate the West Coast. Billy offered to have us come to his parents' farm because they need some help, and he knows we are not troublemakers."

The attendant stared at Midori, Setsuko and May. Just as Midori was about to speak again, he caught himself. Too much, he thought. Maybe I've said too much.

"You need gas?"

"Yes, sir, please fill the tank."

"How do I know you got money? You gotta pay me first."

Midori reached into his pockets. In his right pocket was Thumb-print, and as he caressed the rock, a feeling of calm washed over him. In his left pocket was his wallet. He pulled it out and plucked a ten-dollar bill from inside it and handed it to the attendant.

The attendant snatched the money away from Midori, pirouetted, and headed for the pumps. Midori guided the Coupe over to the tanks where the snarly young man awaited. The trio sat quietly in the car as the pump dispensed a full tank. The display on the pump read $3.60.

"Do you know where the Jones' turkey farm is?" Midori inquired.

The attendant jerked his thumb over his shoulder. "Go to the second dirt road on the right. That's the one. It has a sign on the road. Even you can't miss it."

"Thank you," Midori replied as he waited for the attendant to give him change.

"Well, get going!" the attendant suddenly demanded.

"I'm just waiting for my change and then I'll leave," Midori replied.

"Get lost before I get the hammer and destroy this damn car!"

Midori pulled out of the station, careful to not look back. His hands trembled ever so slightly as he guided his car back onto the road. Not one word was uttered about the encounter. Instead, Midori began intently searching for the dirt road leading to the Jones' turkey farm.

An hour later, Midori was sitting at the Jones' kitchen table drinking a cup of coffee and telling his hosts about the trip from Pasadena as Setsuko and May were bathing upstairs. Frederick Jones was a square-shaped man who looked like the Saturday Evening Post's idea of a farmer. He wore overalls on top of a mildly greasy white t-shirt that revealed a deep tan line on his arms and neck despite it only being March. His wife, Ency, was quick to smile, though less so when she looked at Setsuko than at Midori or May. Ency looked like she wasn't shy about working. Her legs were heavily muscled, and her work boots boasted several layers of dirt.

As Ency made breakfast for the weary travelers, Midori kept offering to help.

"Billy warned us that you wouldn't sit still while we waited on you, and, of course, he was right," Ency smiled. "What else can you tell us about Billy? Tell me, does he have a girlfriend?"

Frederick chuckled. "You ain't got to answer that if you don't want to, young man. Especially if you think it would violate trust between you and young Billy."

Midori smiled. "I can answer it with no problem and without violating any confidence with Billy because I don't know! I only see Billy a few times a year when we work on the yearbooks. We don't go out much as friends because we live about 20-25 miles from each other. But he seems very happy."

Midori stood as soon as he finished eating. "I am looking forward to helping you and Billy's brother in whatever way I can with the turkeys. Please just let me know what you would like me to do. In the meantime, I will wash the dishes. Please tell me where I can find a towel."

At that moment, there was an insistent knock on the door. Frederick glanced, first at Ency, then at Midori, before standing from his chair, pushing away from the table and heading toward the door, his clenched fists firmly planted at his sides.

Frederick opened the door to see three men he recognized standing on his porch. One held a baseball bat in his hand, another quickly removed his hat and held it in his hand while the third kicked mud from the bottom of his feet.

"Chester, Jack, Ike," Frederick nodded. "What can I do for you fine gentlemen this morning?"

"We was just over to the gas station and Emil told us you're harboring some Japs here. That true?"

"Well, now, Chester, I don't know that I'm harboring anyone. I'm no English teacher, but I think that would mean I was hiding them, and I'm not. See?" Frederick opened the door and pointed to Midori, and the newly bathed Setsuko and May. "They're right there. We just fed them and they took baths. Midori over there is a friend of Billy's. He's going to be helping out on the farm. Ever since my back gave out, John's needed some help.

"So, no, we're not harboring any Japs. We've just got a new farmhand is all."

Chester furrowed his brow. "Frederick," he started, but Jack, nostrils flaring, cut him off.

"Listen," the short, squat man said, as he raised the bat over his head, "don't get fancy with us and turn around our words. You know as well as we do that the Japs are poisoning water supplies everywhere they go. You get them Japs outta here or we will, you understand? And if we do, they will have the same damn chance our boys had at Pearl Harbor, you hear?"

"Thanks for stopping by, boys, it's always good to see the three of you," Frederick smiled as he closed the door. Then he turned to face his guests. "Sorry about those boys. I hope that's an isolated incident, and you're not gonna have trouble staying here. We won't let them harm you, but we don't want any trouble either. We gotta live with those jokers long after you're gone."

The next day Midori was combing his hair in the upstairs bedroom where he'd slept in a real bed for the first time in days when he heard another knock at the front door. He opened the door to his room a crack so he could see what was happening. As Frederick opened the front door, Midori caught sight of an angry mob swelling onto the porch and spilling over to cover much of the front yard. His stomach tightened as he thought of Setsuko and May. They wouldn't have left the house, he assured himself.

Frederick held up his hands before placing his fingers in his mouth and blasting out a shrill whistle that momentarily quieted the crowd. "Okay, how about one of you act as the leader and speak?" Frederick requested.

A number of the men stared at their feet and shuffled around, their voices suddenly stifled. Finally, one spoke up: "The Japs gotta go, Frederick! What the hell were you thinking bringing them here? They're gonna poison our water, damn it! You got until tomorrow afternoon to get them the hell out of here, or we will! We ain't kidding, Frederick! We'll burn this damn house down if we have to!! No one wants to hurt you, but this is all your doing. You bring murderers to our town, we will murder them!!"

At that moment, someone in the back of the mob threw a rock that grazed Frederick's scalp and crashed into a decorative vase in the hallway, shattering it to pieces. The tall, sinewy man with the balding pate who had just spoken shrugged his shoulders. "I can't control 'em, Frederick. You all gonna die if you don't get rid of the Japs." He turned to leave, but then returned. "One more thing. Jimmy Jackson knows we're here. Deputies ain't gonna stop us from killing a few random Japs. Just thought you should know that. Tomorrow. Say, 3:00. They better be gone or all hell's gonna break loose."

Midori tried to stop his body from shaking as he slowly opened the door and headed across the hall to find the girls. He knocked on their door and found Setsuko sitting on the bed crying. May stood, uncomprehendingly, at Setsuko's side as they hugged each other. Midori wrapped his arms around both of them.

It's hard to say how long Frederick had been watching them before Midori became aware of his presence and gently pulled away from the others.

"I'm sorry, Midori," Frederick started, but Midori put up his right hand and motioned to Frederick while nodding.

"We understand, Frederick. You have been very kind. If we knew that this was how others in the town would greet us, we'd never have come here."

"Billy is going to be so angry," came Ency's voice from behind Frederick.

"Oh, no, Ency, you did everything you could for us. Billy won't be angry," Midori said, his voice steadying.

"Stay the night they won't be back until tomorrow. The least we can do is feed you well and give you a roof over your head."

Midori looked at Setsuko, who quickly said, "thank you, Ency, we will stay one more night. We are so sorry to put you out. We didn't expect this. We will be on our way tomorrow."

"To tell you the truth," Frederick cut in, "I didn't know what to expect. But, you're Billy's friends. There was never a moment of doubt that we'd try to help you folks out."

The farmer looked down at his feet and kicked an imaginary piece of dirt from the bottom of one. "Where will you go now?"

Midori shook his head. "I don't know, Frederick, but we have a full tank of gas, and our bellies will be full. We will figure it out. Please do not worry; it's not your problem."

Midori slept fitfully. He could hear his sister soothing May more than once during the night and hoped that they weren't disturbing the Jones' whose bedroom was just down the hall in the compact farmhouse.

The morning was consumed with washing clothes and hanging them out to dry as quickly as possible. Frederick headed into what passed for the town and came back with some fruit and vegetables for the trio. Midori pulled out his wallet, but Frederick waved him off. As they were arguing over who would pay for the provisions, there was a sound at the door. The two men looked at each other. The knock was confident, but not belligerent. Frederick headed towards the door and opened it. There stood a solidly built man with a slightly unkempt mane of dark brown hair, very lightly peppered with gray. He smiled and thrust out his hand.

"I'm Oscar. Oscar Hurst. I live down in Blanding, about 20 miles from here. I was over at the Tripp farm helping him out with my thatcher," he said as he turned to face Midori, Setsuko, and May. "I heard you were welcomed quite warmly by the locals," he chuckled.

Midori smiled uneasily and nodded almost imperceptibly as he stood. Hurst sized him up and offered his hand. Midori took the larger man's hand and shook it.

"Not a bad grip for someone as small as you are," Hurst laughed. "You ever work on a farm?"

"Back in high school, I spent the summers in Washington picking strawberries. I did okay with that. One other summer, I worked in a salmon hatchery. But, not on a farm itself, no sir."

Hurst smiled at Midori appraisingly. "Well," he said "people shouldn't treat you the way they did. Not your fault that the Japanese went crazy and bombed Pearl Harbor. Least I don't think it's your fault. Anyway, you are welcome at our farm in Blanding. It's less than an hour away in that Coupe you've got sitting out there. Think about it and let me know," he said as he turned to go.

"Mr. Hurst... "

"Please, call me Oscar."

"Oscar," Midori smiled. "We don't need to think about it. We'd be honored to work on your farm."

Oscar Hurst looked at Midori and grinned. Then he turned to May and Setsuko. "You ladies okay with this plan?"

The two nodded vigorously in tandem as Oscar's smile broadened.

"Man," he grinned, "I can't wait to see the three of you milking the cows!"

ON THE OSCAR P. HURST FARM, SUMMER 1942

BLANDING, SUMMER 1942

CHAPTER TWELVE

Blanding, UT

June 25, 1942

The post office in Blanding consisted of one small room no larger than a kitchen in a medium-sized home. Midori entered the small building flanked by Oscar and Alfreata Hurst. It was Oscar who spoke first.

"Good morning, Sunshine, we're here to register Mr. Shimoda, who's come to live and work with us during this difficult time."

The gray-haired, solid woman behind the lone counter in the room turned without a word and rifled through some papers. "Hah," she said as she slid a paper across her desk, "I knew I'd seen one." "Fill this out and leave it here for me. I'll send it in."

Midori completed the form and handed it back along with a letter to Hede. "Thank you, ma'am," he smiled.

Later that night, Midori stood on the porch and waited for Oscar to come out of the house. It had been three days since George had picked up Setsuko and May to take them to Mapleton, Utah, on the other side of the state, to rejoin the rest of the family. They were going to live with a Mormon family that had offered to sponsor them. Midori had been offered the opportunity to join them but had chosen to stay on with the Hursts.

Well, young man, here you go," Oscar said as he offered Midori a cigarette. "By the way, I know we discussed this briefly, but that was quite a story your brother told about his drive away from the coast. Can you see the three of them taking off their belts and using them to pull the broken down car? What a hoot! Of course, they were probably crapping their pants!"

"Um, I thought Mormons don't smoke or curse?" Midori replied with a small grin.

"I believe we've covered this ground before, haven't we?" Oscar answered as the two men lit their cigarettes and laughed. "You miss Sets and May, don't you, Midori?" he continued.

Midori nodded. "I do, but I also am convinced that I'm better off here. You are very kind to me, Oscar, and I very much enjoy sharing a room with Devon."

Oscar began walking to the far end of the porch. He turned and spoke, "you are an easy man to be kind to, Midori. Joan and Devon already love you like a brother. And, the wife, well, Alfreata may like you more than she likes me!

No woman in your life, Midori? Ever had a serious girlfriend?"

Midori scuffed his shoes on the porch and looked down before looking back up at Oscar. "I was married. Now that I think about it, I still am," Midori smiled.

"Oh?" Oscar replied.

"Her name is Margaret. The night after we got married, she went out to a bar, and I found her dancing with another man when I got there. That behavior continued for a few months, regularly, so I filed for divorce. I haven't seen her for several months now. The divorce process has been slowed down by the war, and by me not being there. So, I guess I'm still married."

"Sounds like Margaret shouldn't have gotten married in the first place," Oscar offered.

Midori nodded. "So," he pivoted, "what will we do tomorrow, Oscar? I mean, besides the usual. Anything out of the ordinary need doing?"

"Ah, Midori, I hate to bring it up, but the barn needs to be cleaned up again, and we may even need to do some roof repairs. Have you noticed that small puddle in the far corner?"

"Yes, Oscar, I meant to speak with you about that. It's not the roof. It's coming up from underneath. I think it's coming in from the side of the barn after a heavy rain."

"Oh? Since when are you a general contractor, Midori?" Oscar smiled. "How did you figure that out?"

"I just dug a bit and traced back. Also, the last time it rained I checked the roof. I'm sorry I forgot to mention it."

"So, now you're apologizing for figuring out the issue with the puddle in the barn? You make me laugh, my friend! You're a handy man to have around the farm."

Midori nodded and sat on the stoop. He looked up at the sky and tried to count the stars, but there were far too many. He stood, extinguished his cigarette, and sat again.

"President Roosevelt is gonna give another Fireside Chat in a few days. He's going to talk about the need for us all to sacrifice," Oscar explained.

"In some ways, the war seems very far away here on the farm, Oscar," Midori replied.

"I don't think it would feel too far away if you tried to drive back to Pasadena, my friend!"

Midori nodded. "I don't think I should try right now," he smiled. "You sound like the voice of reason and experience. I will take your advice!"

"Like I've told you before when it comes to being discriminated against, we've got some experience. And, it's a stupid experience in some ways. I think I told you that our family moved to Mexico when Utah outlawed polygamy to gain statehood. My father had three wives. Crazy, I know."

"But you came back?"

"Well, yes, the Mexicans had no use for a polygamist Mormon family. I was in my twenties and smart enough to know that one wife was more than enough, so I married Alfreata, and we moved to Ogden. Four kids later, we moved here. We needed a lot of hands to operate the farm! Folks around here are LDS and know our shared history so we all get along pretty well."

The two men bantered easily, occasionally smoking between conversations. Eventually, they headed to their rooms to prepare for another day on the farm.

As Midori entered the room he shared with Devon, the teenager put down his book and looked up.

"Devon, you look even bigger lying down than standing up!" Midori exclaimed as he motioned to Devon's feet, which were hanging over the end of the bed by a good three inches.

"I'm taller than dad now, and I don't think I'm done growing," Devon crowed. "Say, are you planning to go back out to Monument Valley this weekend?"

Midori narrowed his eyes and furrowed his brow as he stared intently at Devon, whose dark brown hair made his skin look even lighter than it was. "Did I tell you that?"

"Yes, about two weeks ago, remember? You were mailing a letter to Floyd, and you told me you were asking him to meet you in Monument Valley."

"But, did I tell you the exact date? I thought I just told you generally about the trip?"

"Oh, no, no, you didn't tell me the exact date," Devon replied scrambling to sit up. "I was just thinking that maybe it was this weekend. Are you going this weekend?"

Midori exhaled and folded his arms. "Devon, I need to always be careful nowadays. I trust you, but you know, people just hate me for being Japanese."

"What town are you from again, Midori?"

"Well, it's more of a city. It's called Hiroshima. It's in the southwest part of Japan. Southwest of Tokyo by, maybe about 500 miles. I didn't live there very long. When I was young, my father came to America--to Seattle--and I went to live in Kumamoto with my grandmother. That's even further south and further west. Maybe about 250 miles more. Anyway, no reason you'd ever hear of those places. Probably no Americans know of or ever will know of Hiroshima or Kumamoto."

"Do you miss Japan?'

Midori's face tightened. "No, I don't miss that place at all! I would join the Army—the American Army-- and fight against the Japanese if the Americans would let me! I tried you know. "

"You did?"

"Yes," Midori answered excitedly, "but they wouldn't let me. I'm not a US citizen. And," his voice slowed as he blushed slightly, "I think I'm too small."

"I'm going to join the Army or the Navy as soon as I turn 18 and graduate high school," Devon replied. "My birthday's in December. I'm gonna kill some Germans and some Japs, too!"

Midori appraised his roommate and smiled. "You want to go with me and Lynn Lyman to meet Floyd on Saturday?"

Devon jumped up from the bed. "Yeah, I definitely do," he cried out. "What time will we go? How long will it take us to get there?"

Midori shushed his young friend. "It will take a couple of hours. It's about 75 miles south of here, just over the border in Arizona."

The following Saturday dawned unseasonably hot. The sun blazed its way into the sky as Midori, Lynn, and Devon left the Hurst farm and headed south on US 191. They had a full tank of gas and some sandwiches, which they tried to keep cool by tucking them under the front passenger seat. It was an easy drive, and Midori let young Devon take the wheel. The lanky boy had a heavy foot and Midori had to caution him once or twice, but the trip was otherwise uneventful.

As Devon drove, he glanced over toward Midori. "Where are we meeting Floyd?" he inquired.

"There are two huge rock formations right at the border that look like mittens. We're meeting Floyd in front of the right mitten."

Devon's face betrayed his skepticism. "Mittens, Midori?" he laughed.

Lynn chimed in, "it's true, Devon, they look like mittens. And they provide an amazing photo opportunity. That's why I'm along for this trip. Midori promised to show me some tricks of the photo trade!"

"You will see my young friend, you will see," Midori added. "Monument is one of the most amazing places I've ever seen! I can't wait to get my hands on my camera and take some shots. And, of course, to help Lynn."

At that moment, Midori caught sight of Floyd's car parked up ahead. He reached over and honked the horn loudly, but the sound was swallowed up by the great expanse. Midori quelled the urge to have Devon drive faster and bit the inside of his mouth to deal with his excitement.

Devon pulled the Chevy Coupe alongside Floyd's Chevy and, as soon as the car stopped, Midori jumped out and embraced his friend. "Floyd, so very good to see you!" he exclaimed.

Devon and Lynn joined the two men, and Midori made introductions. "I see what you mean about the mittens, Midori," Devon admitted. "Amazing! Do my mom and dad know about this place?"

"I talked to your dad about the mittens, and he said he'd seen them, yes. But, just seeing them is one thing. Really seeing them, from multiple angles, and with different shadows and lighting, that's what's truly amazing!

"Floyd, how was your drive?"

"It's a long way, Midori! You remember that, right? Two days.

Full days. But, beautiful, scenic, and quiet. So quiet once you leave the coast."

"How are things in California, Floyd?"

"Well, there's a war going on, Midori, you know? People are pretty well consumed with that. There's also this weird age gap of males. There are very few around that are younger than me until you get down to people Devon's age. You know, like no men in their twenties anymore. Makes for a lot of lonely ladies," Floyd smiled.

"I'm joining the Army as soon as I turn 18!" Devon boasted.

"Yes," Floyd smiled, "you and every other 18-year-old. I'm too old; they won't take me. At least not yet. I guess if things don't go well they might grab a few of us over 30 guys."

While Devon and Floyd talked about the war, Midori began to set up his Speed Graphic camera as Lynn looked on.

Recognizing his friend's interest, Midori began to explain the workings of the Speed Graphic. "One of the most important things to do is to set the focal plane shutter speed. You need to first to select a slit width and then a spring tension. For each picture, we must change the film holder, open the lens shutter, set the focal plane shutter, remove the dark slide from the film holder, and then focus and release the shutter."

Lynn squinted as he listened. He had a round mouth that was quick to smile, and narrow, inquisitive eyes. His receding hair-line made his head look larger than it was. He carried an extra fifteen or so pounds on his spindly legs, but his energy was readily apparent.

"Anything I can do to help, Midori?" Lynn inquired.

"Maybe look for good shots," Midori replied as he knelt and then got down on his stomach seeking the best possible angle. He ignored his friends' laughter when they saw him lying on his back and trying to look over his shoulders. Finally, he snapped his first shot. "Okay, Lynn, now we need to change the film holder like I was explaining..."

Midori spent a couple of hours looking for just the right spots from which to shoot. After each shot, he had to go through the lengthy process of changing out the film holder, opening the lens shutter, removing the slide, and refocusing. As a result, he was cautious only to shoot a picture when he was certain that it was going to be worthwhile.

As he neared East Mitten Butte, which was far smaller than its sibling known as West Mitten Butte, Midori spotted some other people. His pace quickened as he drew closer. He saw that they were Native Americans gathered around a small fire. Midori winced at the thought of more heat but realized that they must be partaking in a ritual, not trying to stay even warmer.

Midori slowed considerably as he and Lynn approached the small group. The two men waited a respectful distance away until one of the men in the group turned and motioned to them to approach.

As they reached the group, Midori lowered his gaze and said, "good afternoon. We are very sorry to interrupt. I am Midori, and this is Lynn. I am a professional photographer, and I am hoping to take pictures of many different things today, including the Mitten Buttes."

"Welcome to our homeland," one of the men in the group replied. "We are happy that someone wants to preserve our heritage. You may take pictures of our ritual as well if you would like."

Midori looked up and smiled. "Thank you, that's very kind of you," he replied.

Midori snapped a few shots of the butte as well as several of the Native Americans partaking in their fire ritual. The quartet then took a break shortly before noon as the sun beat down on them. They munched on peanut butter and jelly sandwiches and drank water that was already horribly warm.

"Midori," Floyd began, a twinkle in his big blue eyes, "how do you think William Mortensen would react if I told him you were taking pictures of scenery in Monument Valley?"

"Well, I did take a few shots of the Indians, but, yes, he'd think that Ansel Adams had kidnapped me and made me do it," Midori smiled. "You know, as wonderful as Mortensen was to me, he was a bit eccentric."

"I don't know; I liked all those photos of nude women he had in his studio!"

"You would, Floyd! It's art for art's sake, not some young man's fancy," Midori replied, but he had trouble stifling a laugh.

"Wait, let me get this straight," Devon cut in. "You worked for some guy who got to take pictures of naked women?"

Midori nodded while Floyd and Lynn stifled grins.

"And," Devon continued, "he convinced you and the women that he was taking these pictures for the sake of art?"

Midori nodded again as both Floyd and Lynn turned away snickering.

"Oh, man," Devon continued, now I know why you want to be a photographer! This sounds like the perfect profession!"

"Well, you can start by using that little Brownie camera you have back at the house, Devon. You should have brought it with you today."

"Why, are there naked women who will let me take their pictures somewhere out here?" Devon smirked, sweeping his right arm from left to right in front of him.

The group spent the night camping under the stars. The temperature dropped, but the night was still quite mild, which made for comfortable sleeping conditions. The talk inevitably turned to the war with Devon again exclaiming that he couldn't wait to turn 18 after graduation so he could join the fray.

"What are your plans, Midori?" Floyd asked. "How long do you think you will stay in Utah?"

Midori inhaled deeply and then exhaled very slowly before answering. "I need to go to New York, Floyd, you know that. I want to work with the best photographers in the world. There is much I can learn. And I want to see those tall, tall buildings!

I bet there are some great studios in those buildings, Floyd."

MIDORI'S PHOTO OF MONUMENT VALLEY – SUMMER 1942

CHAPTER THIRTEEN

Blanding, UT September 2, 1942

"Okay, Midori, Devon, let's get a move on," Oscar called out. "Those cows look like they're about to burst!"

Before he could wipe the sleep from his eyes, Midori was hunched over a large cow, his hands working two of its four teats in a downward motion. Milk splashed out into the bowl below, and Midori methodically finished and moved onto the next one.

Devon worked in tandem with Midori, milking the cows in the next aisle.

Oscar sauntered in and laughed. "Man, I wish they could make a movie of this! Midori milks the mama cow! We did a pretty damn good job teaching him, Devon, don't you think?" Oscar winked at his son.

"You don't think Midori grew up milking cows, Dad?" Devon laughed.

"You are both outstanding teachers," Midori chimed in, smiling along with the Hursts. "But, I think Devon still milks two for every one that I milk!"

A half-hour later, after Oscar had disappeared the way he always seemed to when it was milking time, Devon stopped momentarily and joined Midori.

"I have a favor to ask, Midori," Devon began, the mischief in his eyes fighting with his serious tone.

Midori stopped his milking and raised an eyebrow expectantly at Devon.

"May I borrow your car later this afternoon and into the evening?"

"Where are you going, Devon?" Midori asked, caution evident in his voice.

The teenager smiled and looked at his feet. "Just going driving a bit, that's it."

"Oh, who with?"

"Susie," Devon blushed.

Midori reached into his pocket and flipped Devon the car keys. "Be careful," he said.

"I will bring back the Coupe in perfect condition, I promise," Devon replied.

"That's not what I meant," Midori chuckled.

♦ ♦ ♦

September 3rd dawned hot and dry, just like the previous 100 days. Midori was barely awake when he heard the pounding on the front door.

"Okay," Oscar called out, "I'm coming, I'm coming. . . "

Midori cracked the door to the room he shared with Devon just a bit so he could observe Oscar answering the front door.

"Hey, Oscar, sorry to bother you," the man at the door began.

"What's up, LeRoy? How are things in the sheriff's office today?"

LeRoy Wood shuffled his feet and tugged on a strand of hair that stuck up through his cap as he stared at the ground. "Well, it's like this, Oscar," he began his long neck pulling his narrow face up. "We got us a warrant from the US Attorney Dan Shields to pick up Midori for emergency reasons."

"LeRoy, you've met the man, he's harmless. Besides, he's as much of a patriot as you or me," Oscar replied, blocking the door.

"It's not my call, Oscar, now please don't make trouble. Just get the Jap down here, and I'll take him away, and you'll all be fine."

Shaking his head, Midori opened the door. "It's okay, Oscar. Just give me a minute, LeRoy, and I'll be down."

PART THREE

CHAPTER FOURTEEN

Monticello, UT

September 3, 1942

The county jail in Monticello could hardly be called a facility. It consisted of nothing more than a fenced-in hole in the ground. Midori was brought in by LeRoy Wood, who opened the gate and pushed Midori, not in a violent way, but more in a "this is what I'm supposed to do because you're a bad guy" manner.

The stench in the hole was unimaginably vile. Midori glanced toward the far corner. As his eyes adjusted to the darkness, he could make out the profile of a man who appeared to be a Navajo Indian slumped over on the lone bench. Midori had recently spent some time on the nearby reservation, where one of the residents had confused him for a Navajo due to his deep suntan. Midori wrinkled his nose as he became aware of his surroundings. The smell seemed to envelop the man on the bench in much the same way that fog covers a tree in the early morning. Midori stepped toward his new cellmate, then, gently backed away.

"Hey, looks like I got company," the man stood unsteadily as he slurred his words. "Who you?"

"My name is Midori," came the reply. "What is your name?"

"Ah, doesn't matter. Some call me by name. Some call me 'Art.' Some call me 'the Indian,' some call me 'the drunk.' Take your pick."

"I will go with Art," Midori responded, trying to smile. "Arthur is my middle name."

"What are you in for, Midori, being a Jap?"

"Yes, more or less, Art, I think that's it. You?"

"What do you think? I just tol' you, I'm a drunk. Somewhere along the way it became against the law to be drunk in public. Public nuisance they call me. Imagine that? But, why did they say they was throwing you in here with me? Had to have a reason other than being a Jap."

"Taking pictures. And loaning my car to Devon, who drove it out to Cottonwood Creek by the mines to hang out. Vanadium mine, which they think I did."

"Taking pictures? That's it? Hmm. I'd rather be a drunk," Midori's cellmate laughed.

Midori passed the day studiously avoiding deep breaths. The odor was stultifying, the air putrid with human secretions. The monotony was temporarily broken when LeRoy offered the cellmates some stale bread and an odorless, tasteless broth with which to wash it down. For most of the day, however, Midori sat almost motionless, pawing Thumbprint, which he held tightly in his left pocket.

As the tiny bit of daylight visible from the gated front of the hole slipped away, Midori traced the shadows with his eyes. He watched the sunlight fade from the small slat toward the end of what passed for the sheriff's office just outside the jail hole. Half the time Wood got up and left Midori and his hungover Indian cellmate alone. Not that it mattered. There was certainly no way out without a key.

Eventually, Midori realized that he must have fallen asleep because he was awakened by the alternating sounds of his cellmate snoring and moaning. Wood was fast asleep, his feet up on his desk outside the hole holding Midori and the Navajo. Daylight appeared to be breaking, though it was difficult to know for sure. Midori tried to nod off again to no avail.

Not long after he awoke, Midori heard what sounded like voices in the sheriff's office where Wood had been sleeping.

"Sheriff Wood, nice to see you again, Edward Kirby and Walter Foley, Jr. Thanks for holding on to Mr. Shimoda for us. Is he here?"

Wood scrambled to his feet and tucked in his shirt. His impossibly long neck stuck out from his collar and made him look a bit like a goose. "Sure is. I'll rustle him up, fellas."

Wood unlocked the gate and swung it open. "Let's go, Shimoda, FBI's here for your sorry ass."

Midori stood, adjusted his shirt and pants, and shuffled out of jail. Just then, his cellmate called out, "Whoa, FBI! Whooeee!

You must be big time!"

"Shut up, Art!" Wood snapped, his thin face reddening.

"Okay, Mr. Shimoda, I'm Edward Kirby, and this here is Walter Foley, Jr. Like LeRoy just said, we're with the FBI, and we need to ask you some questions."

Midori looked around the room, which doubled as the sheriff's office. He couldn't decide if it was unnaturally bright or if it was just the contrast with the jail hole that made it appear that way. He squinted against the light and nodded to the agents. One of the agents, Midori had already forgotten which was which, motioned Midori to sit on the lone wooden chair that was across from the two, only slightly less uncomfortable looking, chairs where the agents already sat. Wood sat ten or so feet away at his gray, metal desk, picking at his fingers and trying to look like he wasn't paying attention to the goings-on. The incredibly sharp crease in one of the agent's crisp pants—was it Foley--stood out to Midori, and his eyes fixated on it as he noticed the way the cloth dove off of the middle of the agent's leg to each side.

"Young man," the agent began. "You know why we're here?"

Midori looked up and saw by the name badge affixed to his shirt that it was Agent Foley who was addressing him. "Not really, Agent Foley," he began, "no. I mean, well, um, no."

"There was a fire out near one of the vanadium mines the other night," Foley continued in a deep, sure voice. "Several people saw your car out that way. And, we've done some checking around. You've been taking pictures, lots of pictures, and you've not kept us informed of your whereabouts or your personal life

147

in the way we require. You're gonna have to go to the jail in Salt Lake City while we prep for an Alien Enemy Control hearing in front of the board. That's all there is to it."

Midori nodded and then stood, looking expectantly at the agents.

"You got anything to say, Shimoda?" Kirby interjected.

Midori looked at Foley and then at Kirby, whose pants seemed to have enough wrinkles for two agents. Midori shook his head briefly, then stopped. He looked at the ground, then back up. "I haven't used my car in over a week," he murmured.

"Oh," Foley's eyes widened, and his broad forehead creased. "Well, you'll have a hearing, so save it."

"Put your hands behind you, Shimoda," Kirby demanded as he stood, his lean, muscular body unfolding from the chair.

Midori, though standing himself, had to look up at the agents, both of whom were a foot taller than him, and armed with pistols. He put his hands behind him, and Kirby snapped handcuffs in place.

In a matter of moments, the three were walking down the mostly empty street. After ten minutes, they reached a small outdoor area consisting of a few signs and a bench adjacent to train tracks. Kirby and Foley each sat down and motioned for Midori to take the seat between them on the narrow bench.

Midori approached the bench and stared at it momentarily. He then turned slowly around so that his back was facing both the seating area and the agents. He shuffled his feet backward until his hamstrings pushed up against the side of the worn, splintered, wooden bench. He then slowly lowered himself until he was sitting on the bench awkwardly between the two imposing agents.

Less than five minutes after Midori had settled himself on the bench, his hands cuffed behind him, he first heard, then saw, the silver train coming toward them. Midori tried to stand unsuccessfully and fell backward onto the bench grimacing slightly as his backside smacked into the jagged wood. He gathered himself and tried a second and then a third time before finally pushing his legs down hard enough to hoist himself up. He stumbled forward and caught himself just shy of the tracks. Both agents watched with looks somewhere between bemusement and detachment, but neither tried to help.

Once on the aging train, Midori tried to steady himself. He walked down the aisle of the mostly empty car stumbling from side to side like he was drunk. The few passengers seated in the train alternately watched him stumble and averted their eyes. Eventually, Kirby indicated a row that had four empty seats, two on each side of the aisle, and motioned for Midori to sit.

The train lurched forward and then ground to a halt, seemingly stopping more than it went. After a short while, Midori became aware of the stifling heat in the train car. Contributing to this realization was his growing thirst. He inhaled quietly, set his shoulders squarely, and looked straight ahead, trying to ignore the thin film of sweat he now felt on his forehead. It was unusual for Midori to sweat, and the feeling was almost as uncomfortable as the feeling of being handcuffed, though not quite. He focused on the hair of the woman in the row in front of him. Her raven locks tumbled down her narrow back and glistened with moisture.

Foley and Kirby spent some time bantering back and forth about the trip to Salt Lake City, pointedly excluding Midori from the conversation. Midori learned from their conversation that it was a six-hour train trip. He guessed that they were no more than 30 or 40 minutes into it. His thirst continued unabated, though it was intermittently overtaken by his need to pee. He leaned forward slightly and found himself getting woozy. Finally, he spoke.

"Sir," he began, "I'm sorry to bother you, but would it be possible for me to go to the bathroom?"

Kirby looked over at Foley, who nodded. Kirby stood to let Midori get past, but Midori stumbled as he tried to get up. The train was rocking, and Midori couldn't steady himself with his hands behind his back and secured to each other by the handcuffs. Kirby finally grabbed Midori by his shirt and pulled him up. Midori nodded to thank Kirby, who quickly let go of Midori's shirt and wiped his hand on his rumpled pants.

As Midori began walking, the train shook and jostled him into the seat in front of him.

"Hey, off me, Jap!" the raven-haired woman screamed.

"I'm very sorry, ma'am," Midori apologized, "My hands are handcuffed behind me, so it's difficult for me to stand when the train lurches."

"I can see that your hands are handcuffed behind you. It makes me even more unhappy that you touched me, you convict!"

Midori lowered his eyes and walked toward the lavatory, Kirby walking a step behind him. As they reached the door, all eyes in the car were upon them. Kirby reached into his pocket for the key and unlocked the handcuffs.

"You got about two minutes, mister," Kirby indicated, motioning toward the lavatory. Midori rubbed his wrists and quickly opened the lavatory door. As he relieved himself, Midori fished around in his pocket until he found Thumbprint. A bit of tension drained from his shoulders as he rubbed the rock. Midori finished his business and stood in front of the toilet. Now that he'd relieved himself, his thirst began to overwhelm him. He licked his dry, salty lips. Rubbing his hands together, he finally opened the door.

Foley was standing in front of Midori as he exited the lavatory. Somehow, through all the heat and jostling, Foley's pants remained perfectly creased and unwrinkled. The rumpled Kirby stood to the other side and immediately entered the lavatory himself. The two agents took their turns before the three returned to their seats. As the train swayed back and forth, Midori found himself nodding off. He tried desperately to keep his neck upright to prevent himself from touching agent Kirby for fear of the reprisal that he knew would follow.

The train pulled into the station in Salt Lake City just as darkness began to descend. Midori spied the mountains in the distance and smiled briefly in appreciation. As soon as they disembarked, an FBI car pulled up and Foley and Kirby bundled Midori into it for the short ride to the jail on Second Avenue East.

The Salt Lake City jail was a box-like structure, bringing to mind the word "non-descript." Midori stared up at it as the car neared, licking his lips to try to bring some form of moisture to his dehydrated body. Foley, who seemed to do everything with purpose, swung open the door and hustled Midori out of the car and up the steps. Midori slowly scanned the area, noticing a house built almost directly in front of the jail. Foley pushed straight ahead, ignoring the house and headed into the facility, Midori and Kirby trailing in his wake.

Once inside, Midori saw a water fountain next to the men's room. Kirby and Foley were pressing forward, but Midori slowed.

"Please," Midori said softly. "May I use the men's room and get a drink of water?"

"Go ahead," Kirby nodded.

"Thank you, agent Kirby, and, well, sorry to bother you, but. . ." Midori nodded, arching his neck sideways and back to indicate his cuffed hands.

Kirby took a deep breath as he stared at Midori. "Oh, right," he managed a small smile as he pulled the key from his pocket and unlocked the cuffs.

Midori made his way over to the fountain and drank voraciously. He splashed water on his face, and then, looking back at Kirby and Foley, he headed into the men's room. He'd only been inside for ten seconds when the door opened, and both

Kirby and Foley joined him.

In the days following his incarceration in Salt Lake City, Midori began to settle into a routine. Prisoners received food and had an occasional opportunity to bathe. Plus, each prisoner had a cot. Midori shared a cell with three other men, though the makeup of his cellmates was ever-changing, with none seeming to stay for more than a few days. Midori noted the passing of each day by placing a small stone from the exercise yard underneath his cot. He had 13 such stones lined up by the time Robert Landers arrived.

"Geez," said Landers when the guard left him, "you must be real popular in here, little man," he continued, nodding toward Midori as he spoke. Landers was a mountain of a man, with a shock of red hair that rose from his head while at the same time sitting awkwardly atop it.

Midori smiled but didn't respond.

"You a prisoner of war, little man? What'd you do, spy for your mother country?" Landers' voice boomed across the cell and caused the other two men to recoil, though his tone wasn't in the least bit hostile.

"I'm not a prisoner of war, and my mother country is America, just like yours! I do not spy for Japan!"

"Wow, whatsa matter, buddy, did I strike a nerve? You seem pretty worked up by one single question!"

Midori looked at Landers and then down at the ground noticing the man's enormous feet. "I'm sorry," Midori said softly. "I've been in here almost two weeks, and I don't even know what the charge against me is. I don't know how to get myself out of here. I did not mean anything by my small outburst, just a bit frustrated."

"Hey, no problem, little man, I don't blame you! Anyone gives you any grief, you just let me know. I'll take care of you. Hell, I'm in here because I broke a beer bottle over my girlfriend's head," Landers explained, his body shaking as he rolled with laughter at the thought. Once he stopped laughing, Landers turned to Midori. "She kinda deserved it, you know," he explained, "but I don't think the judge wants to see me again."

Midori studied the big man as he spoke. While making sure not to make eye contact, Midori could still see the red spider-like lines in Landers' eyes betraying the fact that he'd been drinking the night before. His hands were enormous and pocked with red dots. They were hands that had seen more than their fair share of activity, some of it undoubtedly violent. Yet, there was a particular, child-like sweetness to Landers, and Midori felt at ease in his presence.

Over the next two days, Midori shared some of his life stories with Landers, and the gentle giant did the same in return. Midori learned that Landers wanted nothing more than to fight the Germans, but he'd been classified as IV-F and found unacceptable for service due to what he said was a heart-related issue. Landers didn't elaborate, but Midori could see in his cellmate's facial expression that it pained him to have to explain his failure to serve. The man also shared his marital history, but it didn't quite add up--a wife here, a girlfriend there.

Just as quickly as Landers had come into Midori's life, he left. On what Midori knew to be Landers' third day in the cell, the guard opened the metal door and nodded at Landers, telling him he was free to go. The big man shook Midori's hand. "Good luck, my Jap friend," he smiled, "good luck."

Midori craned his neck upwards and smiled. "Good luck to you, Robert Landers, good luck to you."

CHAPTER FIFTEEN

Salt Lake City, UT

September 24, 1942

Midori was reasonably certain it was a Thursday when Kirby, still looking slightly disheveled, showed up to escort him to the hearing. Since Kirby didn't advise him to take his meager belongings, Midori assumed he'd be coming back, though nothing was ever certain these days.

Midori had been in jail for nearly three weeks. The early Fall air felt delicious in his lungs, and he breathed deeply many times between the door to the jailhouse and the waiting car. Midori now knew that the house directly in front of the jail belonged to the warden, who Midori overheard bragging about its comforts on more than one occasion. Midori glanced over toward the house, but the curtains were drawn, so the windows revealed nothing of the inside.

It was a short ride to the state-owned building that housed the hearing room. The room itself was no more than a few hundred square feet in size. Midori entered with Kirby who ushered him over to one of two short wooden chairs. Immediately adjacent to the table at which Midori now sat was a similar table that sat somewhat higher off the ground, with two more wooden chairs at which were seated two men in dark suits, both of whom wore white shirts and narrow ties. One man was considerably older and taller than the other and was clearly in charge.

The two tables sat across from yet a third table, which was on a raised platform that made it sit about two feet higher than its lower counterparts. A pale man with an impossibly narrow face sat at this table. He had numerous file folders and wore glasses that were way too big for his pinched nose. As a result, he spent an excessive amount of his time pushing the bridge of the glasses into his face only to have the glasses slide right back down.

Midori stood expectantly in front of his chair. The man at the front table looked down at him and spoke. "Mr. Shimoda, we are here today to conduct an Internal Security-Alien Enemy Control hearing. As you are aware, the Japanese blindsided us and brought us into this war. Due to the manner of their sneak attack, and the general character of the Japanese people, we have no choice but to be very careful in our dealings with those of your race. My name is Gordon Hargrove, and I am a hearing officer with the Federal Bureau of Investigation. Today, I will be in charge of gathering information to present to the Alien Control Board. I am assisted by Mr. Fox.

"We will be hearing from Special Agent Foley of the Bureau, and you will be given a chance to speak as well. We have a hearing stenographer who will capture what we say so that it can be memorialized and shared with others within the government with a need to know both the outcome of this hearing and your whereabouts.

"Now, according to the note in your file from US Attorney, Dan Shields, you were initially arrested on September 3, 1942, and charged with possession of contraband in the form of two cameras and other photographic materials. The authorities found this to be troublesome, and it was the reason for your arrest.

Your situation was compounded by the fire at the vanadium mine near where you were living in Blanding, UT. Your car was seen near that mine by several eyewitnesses on the day of the fire. Not only that, but you also seem to have had a change of marital status that you are required to report to your local draft board, but you have not done so. Additionally, you appear to have done some traveling, which you also are required to report to your local draft board, but you didn't do that either.

"In any event, I've read the documents in the file, and that's what I've learned. I'm now ready to hear from Agent Foley. Mr. Shimoda, you can sit down now."

"Thank you, Mr. Hargrove. For the record, I am Special Agent Walter Foley, Jr. Along with Special Agent Kirby, I've been assigned to investigate Mr. Midori Arthur Shimoda, who is a Japanese Enemy Alien. Mr. Kirby and I picked up Mr. Shimoda from the jail in Monticello, where he was being held, and we brought him to the jail here in Salt Lake. He's now been in custody in Salt Lake for just shy of three weeks.

"As you noted, there are several reasons for concern with regard to the Japanese Alien we are speaking about today. First, and most troubling, is that he's a professional photographer. At the time of the bombing of Pearl Harbor, the alien was engaged in taking photographs at the California Institute of Technology. Complaints were filed almost immediately by local citizens concerned that Shimoda might be taking pictures of sensitive matters at Cal Tech and sending them on to Japan. We've spoken with Mr. Ed Fleck, who is with the Pasadena, California police department. Officer Fleck advised us that he investigated this issue with Cal Tech and determined that the complaints were unfounded.

"We also spoke with Deputy Sheriff Weir of the LA County subversive detail about Mr. Shimoda's connection with a Mr. Harry Hunnewell. Hunnewell had recently inherited several million dollars from his mother, who was from New England. He had a boat and was seen doing things that caused folks to be suspicious. When the LA County detail learned that Hunnewell had been consorting with Shimoda, they conducted an investigation. According to the report filed by Mr. Weir, there was nothing subversive about the relationship. It turns out Hunnewell, just wanted to become a first-rate photographer, and Shimoda was teaching him. It seems it was all above board."

"Okay, Agent Foley, thanks for that background. How about the more relevant matters like the cameras, the fire, the change of marital status, the traveling without notice? All of that?" inquired Hargrove.

The crisply dressed Foley turned to look at Midori, who caught his gaze just briefly before averting his eyes.

"Yes, sir. On September 3rd, Shimoda gave agent Kirby and me full authority to search his room. I believe you should have a copy of that permission in the file, but I can provide it if necessary."

Hargrove waved Foley off. "I've read it," he said, "continue."

"We discovered two Brownie type cameras in the room that the subject indicates he was sharing with Devon Hurst, a 17-year-old boy with whose family Shimoda was living at the time. One camera appears to belong to young Hurst. I'm not sure who owns the other one. Also, Sheriff Wood found the alien in possession of a Kodak camera when he apprehended the subject. Wood took possession of it and gave the subject a receipt for it.

"We don't have much more to report on the fire at the vanadium mine. Shimoda's car was spotted out there. We have three witness statements to that effect in the files.

"Now, as to the travel, well, that's an issue on two fronts. One is the unreported travel itself, but the other is that, on at least one trip, Shimoda was seen taking pictures, which, as you know, we prohibited him from doing. We have here, and you have in your file a report from Mr. Daniel Hayes of Bluff, Utah, that the subject was seen taking pictures in and around Blanding, Utah, and he traveled to Monument Valley, which is 75 or 80 miles away and took pictures there. There are mines on the way there from Blanding."

"Okay, thank you for that, anything else before we hear from Shimoda?"

"Only on the marital status, sir. We don't have much there. Shimoda lists himself as separated, but he never reported that fact to the draft board. That's all we have on that. So, that's the report, sir, please let me know what else you need from us."

"Nothing at the moment, thank you, agent Foley." Hargrove pushed the top of his glasses against the bridge of his nose yet again and turned to Midori. "Please stand, Mr. Shimoda. There are some serious charges here. We need to hear from you."

Midori stood. "Yes, your honor," he replied.

Hargrove waved his arm toward Midori.. "I'm not a judge, Mr. Shimoda. Your judge today, perhaps, but not a judge in reality, so no need to call me that."

"Okay, thank you, Mr. Hargrove. There are many things Agent Foley has spoken about. Does it matter where I start?" Midori asked, a slight tremor in his voice.

"Why not start with the cameras?"

"Yes, sir. There were three cameras mentioned," Midori began speaking quickly. "One was a Brownie that belonged to Devon Hurst, whose room I shared in Blanding."

"Okay, slow down a minute young man, we need to take this all down," Hargrove responded.

"Okay, sorry," Midori replied. "Anyway, I never touched that camera. Then, there was my camera from Pasadena. I think the report may have said that it was also a Brownie, but it was not. It was a Curtis color camera, 5 by 7. When Sheriff Wood came to get me in Blanding, I gave him a copy of the letter I got from US Attorney Shields granting me permission to have and use that camera in Blanding. I wrote to Mr. Shields because I wanted to do some portrait work while in Blanding, and he approved it.

"The Kodak camera you referred to belongs to Mr. Ernest Biggs, the Blanding High School principal. I've never used it. The only time I touched it was to demonstrate to Mr. Biggs how to properly focus," Midori continued, his voice rising.

"Okay, Mr. Shimoda," Hargrove responded, his index finger pressed against his glasses, "I actually believe you're telling me the truth. Any other cameras we need to be aware of?"

"Yes, sir. When I went to Monument Valley, I used a Speed Graphic that my friend Floyd brought for me."

"Keep talking. . . "

"I love the desert. It's my favorite part of the country. So peaceful and so beautiful. Floyd is my best friend. He still lives in Pasadena. Floyd is Caucasian so he didn't need to evacuate. Anyway, he and I planned to meet in Monument Valley so I could take some pictures. I very much miss taking pictures."

"So, you went to Monument Valley on your own without telling anyone?"

"Not on my own," Midori insisted. "I went with Lynn Lyman and Devon Hurst. But, no," he continued more slowly, "I did not report to anyone that we were going."

"Why not, Mr. Shimoda, what were you trying to hide?"

Midori stood as erect as he possibly could. His nostrils flared as he started to speak, but then he caught himself and took a deep breath. "I was not trying to hide anything," he said firmly. "I wouldn't have taken Lynn or Devon along if I had been trying to hide something, sir," he continued more softly. "The fact is that Monument Valley is so far from, well, from everywhere," Midori explained, waving both arms, "that it just didn't occur to me that I had to report that I was going there. It seems like it's another world."

"You taking pictures of the mines out that way?"

"No, sir!" Midori quickly replied, his voice rising. "I was taking pictures of Navajo Indians near the Buttes. I am an honorable man. I know I might look to you like I would be in favor of the Japanese in this war, but I am not!"

"How do we know that's what you were taking pictures of, Mr. Shimoda?"

"Mr. Biggs in Blanding has the pictures. I used the darkroom he set up for me to develop them along with the few portraits I've been able to shoot. I also shot and developed a photo for him that was featured in the 1942 *Piñon*, the high school yearbook."

"Did you go anywhere else outside of Blanding without permission?"

"I requested permission to go to Mapleton to visit my father for Father's Day. When it didn't come through in time, I still drove to see my father, which was about 20 miles away. I was back that night."

"Okay," Hargrove said, gently this time. "That's okay, Mr. Shimoda. Now, what about your marital status?"

"Mr. Hargrove, I am a devoted family man. I married Margaret expecting that she would like to be a devoted family person too. Sadly, that wasn't the case, so I asked her for a divorce. Because of the war, I've had some delays in processing everything."

"Why didn't you report that you have had a change of marital status?"

Midori stood ramrod straight and looked directly at Hargrove. "Because I didn't want to. I didn't want to tell anyone, Mr. Hargrove. I was not proud of what was happening in my life."

Hargrove nodded. "Have a seat, Mr. Shimoda. I need to review my notes before I determine if there's anything further."

Hargrove shuffled through the contents of the file, taking time between each paper to push his glasses up. Occasionally, he'd glance over at Midori.

"Mr. Shimoda, just a few more questions," Hargrove indicated. "Who is Harry Gouldings?"

"Harry is a friend of Floyd's. When Floyd came to meet me at Monument Valley, he stayed with Harry since it's a long way from Pasadena."

"Did you go to Mr. Gouldings' house?"

"For a brief time, yes."

"Did you have a camera while you were there?"

"The Curtis I mentioned. But, Lynn, he had a Recomar camera that he'd brought with him to shoot some pictures at Monument. I showed him some things on that camera while we were at Harry's house, but I never actually used it."

Hargrove looked over the two FBI agents. "Anything further, gentleman?"

"No, Mr. Hargrove, thank you. The record is complete from our perspective."

Agents Foley and Kirby stood and motioned for Midori to do the same. They then escorted Midori back to the jail, explaining that Hargrove would file his report in due course.

Midori breathed deeply as he entered the jail, not knowing when he'd have the opportunity to inhale fresh air again. The warden brought him back to his cell, and Midori was surprised to see the prone body of Robert Landers.

"Hey, Jap boy, I was wondering where you were!"

"You are back?" Midori replied meekly.

"Oh, hell yeah, it's my life little man! In jail Monday, out of jail Tuesday, back by Thursday! Where'd they drag you?"

"I had a hearing about why I'm here?"

"And?"

"I don't know. They will let me know, they said. "

CHAPTER SIXTEEN

Salt Lake City, UT

October 15, 1942

Warden Utrecht took the mail from his assistant and nodded his thanks. His hands were enormous, and even the large manila envelope looked tiny as he pawed it. The warden eventually tore open the envelope and scanned the contents. The report, which was on the letterhead of the Federal Bureau of Investigation, read as follows:

Report made by: J. Gordon Hargrove

Character of Case: Internal Security-J-Alien Enemy Control

Utah File No. 100-3455

On September 3, 1942, Subject MIDORI ARTHUR SHIMODA was apprehended by Special Agents upon authority of Emergency Warrant issued by United States Attorney DAN B. SHIELDS and placed in custody of Sheriff LeROY WOOD, Monticello, Utah.

The Enemy Alien Hearing against Subject was conducted on September 24, 1942 in Salt Lake City.

Utrecht skimmed over the summary of the accusations against Midori and eight others being held for similar violations. He continued reading near the bottom of the page:

*Subject's appearance before the Board is due to his apparent posses-
sion of (a) camera. This boy is physically frail, but of an artistic
and very sensitive nature. He is high strung. He had difficulty in re-
straining tears. He feels discouraged. He came to America where (sic)
he was nine years old. He stated that it is difficult for him to look at
himself as an alien. . . He was evacuated from Lower California and
had bad luck in choosing Monticello, but in order to make no trouble
he went to Blanding where he was happy until picked up. . .Blanding
is far from the maddening crowd. It is a remote agricultural and cattle raising community far in the southeastern corner of the state; has
few people – far from any railroad or any defense or war activities. It
has no saloons, and not even beer is sold there. It is a country of magnificent distances. Subject said it seemed to (sic) rural and so peaceful
that it was hard to remember that he was an alien cut off from the use
of a camera.*

*He represents one of the many individual tragedies of the war. We
think he is not in the least dangerous. He should be allowed to return
to Blanding if this arrest by the F.B.I. has not made it impossible for
him to stay there.*

*We recommend that he be paroled under sponsorship as soon as pos-
sible so that his spirit may not be broken.*

Two hours later, Midori was summoned from his cell and told
to gather his belongings. He nodded to Landers and the others
in the cell and headed out with the deputy toward the warden's
office.

"Mr. Shimoda, as you know, I am Warden Utrecht. I've got here
on my desk the report from Mr. Hargrove about your hearing.
Mr. Hargrove has recommended parole for you. He determined

that you are not a threat to the safety of our country. But, there are a few requirements. We are giving you what amounts to a conditional release under sponsorship. This gentleman here," Utrecht said, motioning to his left, "is G.S. Berryman. He's agreed to be your sponsor."

Midori nodded slightly and then faced Berryman. "Thank you, Mr. Berryman, I am very appreciative."

Berryman had but a wisp of white hair on top of his pink skull. His smile was quick and broad. "Glad to help, Midori, glad to help," he said.

Utrecht continued, "you must report to Mr. Berryman at least once each month, Mr. Shimoda. And, you are on parole, not totally free, so you must also report in to your parole officer, Otto Mutz, once a month on the 25th. Here's his information," Utrecht said as he handed Midori a small card. "I think Mr. Berryman has an idea or two as to where you can find a place to live and some work. Do you have any money, Mr. Shimoda?"

"Yes, but it's being held back in Blanding by Mr. Parley Redd. He owns the general store and the only one in town with a safe. I have $300 in defense bonds and over $100 in cash. I also have a car and the rest of my clothes in Blanding."

Utrecht looked over at Berryman, who quickly stated, "we'll get you settled, Midori, and then we'll get your money, your clothes, and your car. Let's get you a bath and a solid meal!"

CHAPTER SEVENTEEN

Salt Lake City, UT

December 23, 1942

"Midori, why did you tell that customer we'd have her pictures developed by tomorrow, you know we already have more work than we can handle?" Richard Stokes, the owner of Stokes Photography Studio, asked. Richard wasn't much taller than Midori, but he outweighed his employee by at least 50 pounds. He insisted on wearing a tie every day, whether he was working or simply relaxing at home.

"Mr. Stokes, I will stay late to finish the developing and all of the retouching of the negatives that still needs to be done. It's very important to people that they have their pictures for Christmas."

"Richard," G.S. Berryman called out to his cousin, "normally I would stay late too, but I promised Mildred I'd go shopping with her to get the last few gifts for the kids. But, you know, Midori could close up."

Richard walked to the corner of the small studio and straightened a picture hanging on the wall, all the while appraising both his cousin, with whom he owned the studio and Midori. Before he could speak, G.S. continued. "Midori has been in my custody for over two months now. He's a model citizen, Richard; you know that. He's just trying to satisfy the darn customers," G.S. smiled.

Richard finished straightening the picture, stood back and looked at it, and then nodded. "I suppose there's no harm. Midori, I will lock up. You can let yourself out the back and pull the door shut. It will lock after you. How long do you think you will be here?"

Film in need of developing and pictures awaiting pick up packed the shop. Midori looked around at the clutter and thought for a moment. "No more than three more hours," he said confidently.

"Three more hours," Richard bellowed. "I, well, I . . . "

Midori quickly waved him off. "Mr. Stokes, I am not expecting you to pay me for the extra time; I will just do the work. Please, do not worry."

Richard looked at Midori with a blank expression on his face. He pursed his lips and cocked his head to the left. He began to speak and then stopped. Finally, palms facing up, he said, "no, no, that's not right. I won't have someone work for me and not get paid. Keep track of the overtime. Please."

Several hours and numerous developed and retouched photos later, Midori tidied up his work area and prepared to leave. He realized for the first time how hungry he was and tried to remember what food he might have at his apartment. No shops would be open at this late hour. He stepped out the back door into the alleyway and made sure that the door locked behind him. As he started to walk towards Main Street from the back of the shop, he quickly became aware of a hulking figure standing at the end of the alley blocking the way to Main Street. With the back door locked, Midori had no choice but to approach and try to get around the mass of humanity in front of him.

"Excuse me," Midori said quietly as he neared the imposing man, but the unsuspecting figure was startled and whirled around.

"Well, if it ain't the Jap!" Robert Landers cried out.

"Oh," Midori laughed, relief evident in his voice.

"What exactly are you doing, Midori? You know, people think that Japs are sneaky to begin with, why are you hanging around in the alleyway?"

Midori motioned to his left and said, "I work in the studio right there. I was working late and had to let myself out the back," he continued as he pointed in the direction of the door.

Landers looked impressed. "So you got a job? That makes me feel bad. I can't seem to get a job, but a Jap like you gets one."

"Robert," Midori began, but the big man cut him off.

"I know what I gotta do. Still, when a Jap gets hired before a drunk, you just hafta wonder."

"Good luck, Robert, I hope to see you again. Oh, and Merry Christmas."

"Holy crap, is it Christmas? Damn!"

"Well, not yet. Tomorrow is Christmas Eve. So, I was a bit early, but just the same."

"Do Japs celebrate Christmas, little man?"

"Some do, some don't, Robert. It's not a matter of country but religion. I'm a Christian, so I celebrate it, but others are Buddhists, and they may not."

Landers rubbed his huge paw of a hand on his head and squinted. "Well, then, Merry Christmas, Midori. I hope you get some good presents," he laughed.

Midori nodded, smiled, and pushed on past Landers. He turned right on Main Street and walked briskly past the mostly well-lit, decorated shop windows. All in all, it was a subdued Christmas, though it certainly seemed more festive than the prior year's.

Midori turned left onto South Street and headed toward State Street. Midway down the block, he stopped at a two-story brick building with the number 100 posted on the front door and headed inside. The stairway directly in front lead upstairs to the apartment Midori shared with George Yamate. Midori tacked to the right as he headed upstairs. The stairway was wide enough to accommodate four people easily, and it was long, too, at 20 or so steps.

Midori reached the top of the landing and headed down the

hall. He walked straight past his apartment door to the bath-room at the end of the hall. After finishing there, Midori headed back to his apartment. On the way back, he passed the Yama-shita's apartment. Masakichi Yamashita was the patriarch of the family while Asano, his once-picture bride who was twenty years his junior, was similar in age to Midori and his roommate, George. The Yamashitas had four children, June, who was 16, Ted, who was 12, Susie, who was ten, and Sab, who was eight. Masakichi had been married before but his first wife had tragic-ally died during the flu epidemic of 1918, and their son, Jay, had died equally as tragically by drowning in the irrigation reser-voir behind their house when he was just a toddler.

Midori stopped for a moment in front of the Yamashita's apart-ment as he heard a young girl's voice singing:

There's a song in the air
But the fair senorita doesn't seem to care
For the song in the air.
Oh, I'll sing to the mule
If you're sure she won't think that I am just a fool
Serenading a mule.

Midori smiled as he listened to Susie Yamashita crooning the words to "The Donkey Serenade." His smile widened as he im-agined the beautiful Jeanette MacDonald riding in her stage-coach and being serenaded by Alan Jones on horseback riding along next to her. Ah, what a scene!

Midori opened the door to his apartment to see his roommate George lounging on his bed, reading a book. George looked up, stretched his lean arms over his head, smiled, and spoke.

"Wow, you're late! Where you been?"

"Working. I promised some pictures would be ready by Christmas."

"Hmm. You getting extra pay?"

"I think so. They, well, that is, Mr. Stokes, said yes."

"Ah, well, he's the tight one! G.S. won't get in the way of that. Say, the little ones were over again."

"I figured that might be the case. I was walking back from the bathroom and heard Susie singing "Donkey Serenade! Meantime, I'm starved. Any food left around here?" Midori asked as he made his way toward the small kitchen. The entire apartment consisted of one room. The roommates each had a bed that hugged opposite walls. A small, somewhat creaky wooden table and two folding chairs sat near the front door to the immediate right of which was what passed for a tiny kitchen.

"A bit of tsukemono. Maybe some rice to go with it. Tea."

Midori scraped together some dinner, which he ate at the table. George joined him for a bit before they both headed to bed. Tomorrow was going to be a hectic day.

Christmas Eve day was a bustling affair at the Stokes Photography studio. Midori had finished every last project the night before, so the three men spent most of the day showing their customers the finished products and then wrapping them.

Shortly before closing time at 5:00 G.S. and Richard approached Midori.

"Midori," Richard began, "We can't thank you enough for the great work you've done since you got here, but specifically these last two weeks. You helped make Christmas special for many people through your hard work and determination. Are you sure you won't join us tonight at G.S.' house for Christmas Eve? We have a fine goose dish, I hear!"

Midori smiled and shook his head. "Thank you, but no. My roommate George and I are having dinner together, and then the two little ones from across the hall will come over to play, and we will celebrate with them. They are like family to us, so we won't be lonely."

With that, Richard nodded to G.S., who pulled out an envelope and handed it to Midori. "Your regular wages are in here, Midori, plus overtime for the other night."

"And," Richard smiled, "a well-earned bonus! We hope you will be with us for a long time, Midori."

Midori walked home through a light blanket of snow. Wreaths hung on many doors both in recognition of the holiday and to honor the men and women serving the country. Midori wondered how long the effort would last. Information was somewhat scarce though it seemed like the war was beginning to turn toward the Allies a bit more than earlier. Still, Midori couldn't help but think it might be a very long time before peace would descend. Selfishly, he wondered what that meant for him, before pushing the thought away and reminding himself to be thankful that he was a free man this Christmas.

Midori kicked off the snow and stepped inside The Elms Hotel. A Christmas tree with some fake presents beneath it brightened the drab foyer, but that couldn't hide the fact that the building was slowly decomposing. Paint chipped off the ceiling, bubbling where water had damaged it. Much of the carpet in the hallway leading to the stairs was now threadbare.

The Elms was one of the very few apartment buildings in Salt Lake to serve the Japanese community. Japanese workers who came to America to work on the railroads shortly after the turn of the century eventually made their way from the West Coast to Salt Lake City. In 1902 the E.D. Hashimoto Company was formed in Salt Lake as a labor agency to help men find jobs and housing in return for a portion of their salaries. By 1906 over 13,000 Japanese men were working on America's railroads; however, harsh anti-Japanese sentiment lead to Japan slowing the tide of immigrants to the US in 1908 under the so-called Gentleman's Agreement. Those who stayed eventually moved into other professions, but most lived in places called "Japantown." The Elms Hotel was located in Salt Lake City's Japantown, and, when Midori moved in, it was a holdover from that earlier era.

Midori took the stairs two at a time and got to the apartment door only slightly out of breath. He turned the handle and immediately saw Susie and Sab playing on the floor. Susie jumped up and ran toward Midori, her pigtails bouncing behind her. She hugged Midori's leg with her long, though impossibly thin, arms.

"Merry Christmas, Susie," Midori called out and handed the perfectly dressed little girl an impeccably wrapped gift in a long, narrow box. Suddenly, Sab, seeing that his sister had gotten a gift, jumped up to hug Midori as well. His grip was surprisingly strong for such a little boy.

"You don't have anything for little boys, do you, Midori?" George smirked.

Sab, looking crestfallen as Midori hid his hands behind his back, began to release his stubby arms. Just as the boy's lips began to quiver, Midori pulled his arms around and handed Sab an equally perfectly wrapped box. "Merry Christmas, Sab!" Midori smiled.

"Thank you," Sab blurted out, "You very sweet!"

"Hey," George called out to Midori while chuckling at Sab's difficulty with pronunciation, "where's mine?"

Midori laughed at his angular roommate, still lounging on his bed. "I got you the same gift as you got me, just as we agreed!"

Just then, Susie stood up, adjusted her crinkly plaid dress, and said, "please, can you play "The Donkey Serenade?"

Midori walked over to the record player and turned it on. Within seconds, Alan Jones was singing, and Susie was singing right along with him, performing as though she were the lead actress, and the small apartment was her theatre. Sab began dancing around the room in a somewhat spastic fashion as the quartet filled the space with laughter. Before long, the door opened, and Susie and Sab's mother, Asano Yamashita, and their two other siblings, June and Teddy, came into the room carrying cake and cookies. The group enjoyed a festive Christmas Eve party with "The Donkey Serenade" playing over and over to Susie's delight. The adults and older children quickly tired of it but were unsuccessful in having it turned off.

THE DONKEY SERENADE
from the MGM Motion Picture Musical THE FIREFLY

By RUDOLF FRIML
and HERBERT STOTHART

First performed in the 1937 musical " the Firefly" , "The Donkey Serenade"   remained
popular for decades.

CHAPTER EIGHTEEN

Salt Lake City, UT

April 20, 1943

Midori was cleaning up the back of the shop when Richard Stokes approached him. "There's been a slight change of the schedule for the rest of the week, Midori," he explained.

Midori arched his eyebrow just slightly and continued straightening the items on the table. "Oh?" he said.

"I won't need you to do the Simpson Easter shoot after all, they've changed things up."

Midori looked impassively at his boss. It was the third time in as many days that Richard told Midori he wouldn't be needed on a shoot. Each time Mr. Stokes had made up some excuse or another, but it wasn't hard to see through them.

After locking up the store with Richard, Midori headed toward the Elms Hotel. But, on this night, he walked past the entrance away from downtown. Within a few short blocks, he found himself in a quiet, residential area with few people on the streets. Midori slowed to look at a battalion of yellow and white daffodils. He stooped and gently took one between his thumb and forefinger. He inspected the stem and then the flower before gently releasing it, standing, and moving on.

Midori took a deep breath as he looked around. There were certain things he would miss about Salt Lake, others he would not. Daffodils fell in the first category. Bigots who wouldn't let him work fell into the second. As Midori wandered the streets, he could hear Grandma's voice. "You are a Shimoda, Midori. A descendant of Samurai. One day, we will return to our former glory. One day we will again be who we are meant to be." Midori nodded. Yes, he thought. The modernization had ended the days of the Samurai, but that didn't mean we Shimodas couldn't regain our glory by other means.

The sometimes wonderful, other times annoying, "The Donkey Serenade" was blaring through the door and into the hallway as Midori approached the apartment. He turned the knob and Susie ran over to hug him. Midori squeezed her small body against his leg as a barely perceptible tear moistened his eye. George looked up from his bed where he'd been reading to Sab, and registered concern at his friend's mien, but Midori quickly waved him off.

Eventually Susie and Sab headed across the hall to their apartment, and George pounced. "What's wrong, my friend?"

Midori took a deep breath, looked at his roommate and friend, and then turned away silently. After a few minutes, he turned back and looked again at George.

"I am going to New York, good friend."

"Huh?" George responded, his nose crinkling. "Have you gotten permission from the FBI or INS or whoever you need to get it from?"

Midori stared intently at his friend. "No, I have not," he replied.

"What about your boss, don't you need to keep him informed of your whereabouts at all times or something like that?"

"Technically, I only have to check in with him once every thirty days, but I see him almost every day at work."

"What does he think of your plan?"

Midori looked down and then met his friend's gaze. "I have not told him. I will tell him tomorrow. George, I am wasting my time here. I know you will understand me when I tell you that I must go to New York to test myself. To see how I compare to the great photographers in one of the greatest cities in the world. I need to find out, George. I must know the truth. Shinjitsu."

George stood from his bed. He towered over his shorter roommate, so he tried to stand back so as not to intimidate him. George narrowed his eyes and ran his hand through his wispy, jet-black hair as he appraised Midori, who met his gaze without wavering.

Finally, George spoke. "I understand, Midori, but, how do you think ol' Berryman is going to react? You think he's going to just smile and say, 'have a nice trip'?"

"To be honest, my dear friend, George, I don't care. I am wasting my time here. They won't even let me take simple portrait photos. They are all afraid of me here, George. Like I am going to do something horrible during a photo shoot. I mean, really? Crazy to think that way. I need to go to New York where there won't be so much hatred, and where I can learn once and for all how I compare to the great ones."

George scratched the right side of his head with his left hand, which made him look both thoughtful and goofy at the same time. He dropped his hand and said, "Midori, do you understand that it may not be up to you whether you go to New York or not?"

Midori stood his ground. "I'm going to New York, my friend. One way or another."

Midori slept fitfully that night and was up before dawn. He boiled some water on the hot plate and sipped quietly on his tea as he watched his roommate sleep. Shortly after, he slipped out of the door and meandered along the silent streets of Salt Lake City. Easter was just a few days away, and the Spring morning was warmer than the previous day had been. Midori scanned the facades of the houses as he walked. He stopped briefly to admire a small, brick home surrounded by daffodils and another, purple, flower that Midori couldn't quite place. He noted with appreciation the care the owners took in their plantings. Even more wonderful was the way the owner had surrounded the flowers with a rock garden. Midori was stunned by the harmony created by the rocks and flowers; the alternating colors and sizes; the way the elements were perfectly situated.

As he continued Midori smiled at the completely haphazard nature of the next home's appearance. A few straggly flowers mixed with an abundance of weeds. "My life is like this house at the moment," Midori thought. "I am like one of those flowers mired in an area, not to my liking and surrounded by weeds. I need to get to New York," Midori determined, "so I can arrange my life to be like the last house. Orderly. Attractive. Under control. In charge."

Midori wondered, not for the first time, about the impact of the war on him. He felt selfish for thinking about such a global catastrophe in such personal terms. Still, if the war continued unabated for years, Midori feared he'd be too old to ever work as a photographer in New York. If it ended very soon with a victory there'd be a flood of Caucasian men coming home as heroes and they'd take every last job. No one would want him then either. And, if the war ended in defeat, well, that would be bad for everyone involved. Now was the time, Midori knew, to seize what might be his one last opportunity. Like a Samurai.

At 9:00 AM sharp Midori turned the handle on the front door of Stokes Photography and entered the shop. He greeted his two bosses, took off his lightweight jacket and got down to work. The day passed uneventfully as the trio worked to fill the Easter picture orders. Berryman and Stokes left for a while to do a photoshoot---one they had uninvited Midori to attend. When they returned, Midori approached G.S. Berryman.

"G.S., may I speak with you for a minute?"

"Of course, Midori, you don't need to ask permission to speak to me," G.S. smiled. "What's on your mind?"

"I am going to be quitting my job here, G.S.."

Midori's boss suddenly stopped smiling and creased his brow. He spread his legs a few inches further apart and fixed his gaze directly on Midori. "Have we not treated you well, Midori? Do you have a job offer you consider better?"

"Oh, no, no, no," Midori quickly countered. "You have treated me very well, but I am going to New York."

G.S. reacted as though he'd been pushed, staggering back a full foot before regaining his balance. He composed himself and then spoke. "You have a job lined up?'

"I do not," Midori replied.

"How about permission from your parole officer, Mr. Mutz?"

"I've not spoken to him about it. My next report to him is due on Easter."

"You planning to ask his permission?"

Midori looked at his feet before raising his head and meeting G.S. Berryman's eyes. And, though he met his boss' gaze, Midori did not answer the question Berryman had posed.

◆ ◆ ◆

Good Friday dawned unusually warm. Midori left his jacket at home and set out for his early AM pre-work walk. He had checked on the Coupe the previous evening, and it was running fine even though he hardly ever used it. His frustration mounting, Midori tried to decide if he should hop in the Coupe and start heading East or if he should finish working the two weeks he'd promised Berryman and Stokes. He wrestled with the options as he walked along, conducting his usual inspection of everything from Spring flowerbeds to crumbling facades. Hanging over it all was the fact that he had to report to his parole officer, Otto Mutz, on the 25th. Midori was a man of honor and not one to lie. So, that was it. His mind was now made up. He would be honest with Mutz and would work through the final days of the two-week notice he'd given. He would leave for New York on May 7th or 8th. With that Midori strode resolutely to work and greeted his co-workers.

Had it not been for the backlog of orders promised for Easter, he would have closed the shop for Good Friday, Richard Stokes advised. And, showing he meant it, Stokes did close at 2:00 PM when the promised orders were completed.

Midori wished his colleagues a Happy Easter and walked out

the door of Stokes Photography, and headed toward the Elms Hotel. He knew that George wouldn't be home yet and relished the thought of some alone time in the apartment. Much as he loved his roommate and the kids from across the hall, Midori was starved for alone time. He walked through the front door of the Elms Hotel and was startled to see his muscular parole officer, Otto Mutz, standing in the lobby.

"Midori, we need to talk," Otto said solemnly.

"Yes, Otto, we can go to my apartment."

CHAPTER NINETEEN

Salt Lake City, UT

April 25, 1943

Midori awoke on Easter morning in a jail cell just down the hall from the one he'd inhabited the prior year. He wasn't angry at G.S. Berryman for contacting Otto Mutz, or Mutz for contacting his superiors. They all had a vested interest in knowing Midori's whereabouts at all times as they'd accepted oversight of him. His plans to go to New York had unnerved them. If anything, Midori blamed himself for underestimating the situation.

The morning passed slowly at first, but then the bow-legged deputy came to Midori's cell and said, "Shimoda, you have some visitors." He unlocked the cell door and continued, "come with me."

Midori followed the deputy, his eyes darting between the man's bizarre gait and the other cells. Some of the cells were empty, others occupied by men, all men. Some of the prisoners sat on the three-legged stools that each cell contained. Others sat on the floor, their backs leaning against the wall. The deputy walked quickly on the outside of his feet and led Midori into a large, open, well-lit room where other prisoners were engaging with visitors. Before he could fully get his bearings, Midori saw a young Japanese girl with lustrous black hair running toward him. He smiled as Susie wrapped herself around his leg, and Sab followed close behind.

Midori broke out into a huge grin as he saw George with Susie and Sab's sister, June, and their mother, Asano. He tried to walk over toward them, but Susie was clinging so tightly to his leg that he found himself almost dragging her along. Laughter filled the room as they shuffled towards his other visitors.

Before long Susie and Sab were involved in a game with the other children visiting prisoners. Midori sat and chatted with George and Asano until he noticed that June was standing a few feet away, not seeming to know what she should do. At just shy of 17 she was too old to play with Susie and Sab, but too young, perhaps, to be involved in discussions with the adults.

Midori stood and walked over to June. "How are you doing, June? Are you having a nice Easter?" he inquired with a smile.

June looked down for a moment and then met Midori's eyes. She blushed slightly before replying, "I am fine, Midori, I'm sorry they put you in here," she continued while sweeping her right arm in front of her.

"Your Easter dress is very pretty, June," Midori replied as he watched her quickly lower her arm.

"Thank you, my mom sewed it for me."

The longer the visit continued, the more animated it became. Eventually, it was time for the group to leave.

"What's the plan, Midori, do you know?" George inquired.

"They say I will have a hearing or something soon. Violation of parole I guess," Midori shrugged.

"What can we do to help, my friend?"

Midori shrugged again. "Come back soon," he smiled. With that, he walked back to Asano and June and hugged them each good-bye. No one seemed in much of a rush to bring Midori back to his cell, so he stood and watched as George, Asano, June, Susie, and Sab headed for the door. The dress did look lovely on June, Midori thought. Asano had done a wonderful job of sewing it.

CHAPTER TWENTY

Salt Lake City, UT

May 3, 1943

It was the middle of the night when Midori became aware of his cell door opening. He'd been alone in the cell since his arrival, but that was apparently about to end. He glanced up from his bed to see the deputy leading a lumbering oaf of a man into the cell. Robert Landers had returned.

"Hey, it's you!" Landers cried out. "Why are you back?"

Midori smiled wanly. "It's the middle of the night, Robert. Can we discuss this tomorrow?"

The big man snorted. "Why you afraid you will be too tired to go to work tomorrow?" he snickered.

"The US Attorney is coming to give me a re-hearing tomorrow to see if they are going to keep me. I need to be ready. Please let me sleep."

Landers' face grew serious. "US Attorney? Are you some kind of big deal that the US Attorney would come all the way here to talk to you?"

Midori took a deep breath and exhaled slowly. "Robert, we need to sleep. But, there are many US Attorneys. They are in many different cities. The guy who is coming to see me isn't *the* US Attorney; he's one of many. Now, please, go to sleep."

Midori was happy to realize he'd fallen back to sleep when the guard came to get him at 8:00, but he didn't understand what the guard was doing there so early. The hearing was scheduled for 11:00, so Midori followed the guard to the visiting room, unsure of what lay ahead. As he approached the wide-open room he saw his roommate, George. The guard opened the door and let Midori in and then turned back.

"Shouldn't you be at work, George?" Midori asked.

"Heading there now," George replied. "But, first, the Yamashitas made you this," George said as he handed Midori a small box decorated with painted flowers of yellow and purple.

"It's beautiful, please thank them, George."

"We all wish you good luck at the hearing, Midori!"

George's visit left Midori feeling calm, and it carried over until the guard came back to get him shortly after 11:00. Midori's stomach tightened as he arranged his short black hair with his hands and walked behind the guard to the other side of the prison. He reached into his pocket to assure himself that Thumbprint was safely in there, and then let his hands fall near his hips. The guard brought Midori into a room he'd never seen before. It was small, maybe 10 x 12, and painted an impossibly bright white. The light bulbs were uncovered and of a high enough wattage that they shone off the walls, thereby enhancing the effect of the whiteness. A single metal table was centered in the room with four chairs attending it. Two were on one side and one on the other. The fourth was at the head of the table, while the foot of the table was empty.

Midori recognized everyone in the room except the court reporter who stood near the back until the door opened and she was handed a chair.

Seated at the head of the table was Dan Shields, the US Attorney. He was just shy of 6 feet tall, with wispy, sand-colored hair and piercing blue eyes. His skin was taut across his face, though he was quick to smile. FBI agent Edward Kirby sat to Shields' right, and Midori's parole officer, Otto Mutz, sat next to Kirby.

The men exchanged quiet greetings and then Shields spoke. "Mr. Shimoda, I can't say any of us are happy to be here, but, here we are, nevertheless."

Midori alternated between making eye contact with Shields and looking down at the table in front of him. He rubbed Thumbprint for comfort and luck.

"At this point, I will bring this rehearing to order. Mr. Edward Kirby, with the FBI, is here. Mr. Kirby will be able to fill in the information we may need from the earlier hearing as he represented the government at that time, along with Mr. Foley. For the record, we will state that Mr. Mutz is your parole officer, and will be giving testimony in that capacity. Before we get going, do you have any questions, Mr. Shimoda?"

"No, Mr. Shields, I do not."

"Okay, then Mr. Mutz, we will take your testimony. Please advise us as to the nature of your concerns related to the enemy alien."

Otto Mutz was dressed impeccably in a gray suit with a white shirt. He had a perfectly tied red bow tie pulled up tightly against his shirt collar. His heavily muscled body made him appear taller than he was, so it was still somewhat jarring when he spoke in a high-pitched squeal.

"Thank you, Mr. Shields," Mutz began, and Midori could see Shields cringe from the parole officer's voice. "This is a curious case. Mr. Shimoda has checked in with me each month as required by his parole, for, let's see, six months. April would have been the seventh. He's been, frankly, a model citizen. He's worked at Stokes Photography Studio the entire time and been in the personal custody of G.S. Berryman, a fine gentleman. Mr. Berryman noted no problems with Mr. Shimoda during his employment until about two weeks ago. At that time, Mr. Shimoda told Mr. Berryman that he was quitting and moving to New York. Mr. Berryman, as his custodian, became concerned and eventually determined that he needed to tell me about Mr. Shimoda's ideas."

As Mutz paused for a drink of water; Shields glanced over at Midori, who looked back impassively. Shields looked back at Mutz and motioned for him to continue.

"Well, as soon as Mr. Berryman shared his concerns with me, I sought out Mr. Shimoda and found him coming into his residence in Japantown at the Elms Hotel. Mr. Shimoda then told me the very same thing he'd said to Mr. Berryman, that he was going to New York. I asked him why, but his answer wasn't satisfactory at all, so I contacted my boss, and here we are." Mutz folded his powerful arms across his chest and gave a self-satisfied grin in the direction of Midori.

Shields leaned back in his chair. The light from the uncovered bulb glinted off the metal of the US Attorney's chair and reflected on the white walls. Midori watched as that played out and waited for Shields to continue. Finally, the lanky US Attorney looked over at Midori and allowed the front of his chair to rest on the floor. "So," he began, "we seem to have something of a stalemate here, Mr. Shimoda, don't we?"

"I'm sorry, stalemate?" Midori answered.

"Well, you insist you're going to New York, but we aren't about to let you go just because you say that's what you want to do. So we have a problem. We need more information, Mr. Shimoda, that's what we need. What do you intend to do in New York, Mr. Shimoda?"

"I am a photographer," Midori replied.

Shields leaned back in his chair again. "We know that Mr. Shimoda, that wasn't my question. What do you intend to *do* in New York? Do you have a job lined up?"

"No, sir, I do not."

"Then why must you go there? Got a girl?" Shields smiled.

"No, Mr. Shields, no girl," Midori replied softly.

"Then why on earth did you decide after six months of being a perfect employee that you were going to quit and head to New York? I just don't get it."

"I must go, Mr. Shields. It's for reasons personal to me."

"So you say. You've said the same damn thing to Mr. Berryman and Mr. Mutz. Now, Mr. Shimoda, I'm going to tell you something. I think you are a very bright man. I'd hire you if I needed a photographer. But I wouldn't do it if you weren't honest with me. So, if you want me to ever hire you as a photographer, or, more importantly, to let anyone else hire you as a photographer, *ever,* then tell me, what the heck is so dastardly critical that you must go to New York now?"

"Mr. Shields, my reasons for needing to go are very personal to me. They have nothing to do with the war or anything else you might be concerned about. They relate solely to my career, I assure you."

"If you want to assure me, then tell me what you are planning to do in New York!" Shields thundered.

"I am sorry Mr. Shields, I am not trying to be difficult. My hope is to one day be a photographer in New York. I know that I am restricted from using a camera outside of the studio right now, but I want to work in a studio in New York."

"Why now, Mr. Shimoda, what is so crucial about now?"

"Because I feel the time is right, Mr.; Shields. My reasons are deeply personal. It goes back to when I was living in Japan with my grandmother. When I was a little boy."

Shields leaned back on his chair and stared at Midori. Then he looked at the court reporter. "This is off the record, please." The reporter nodded, and Shields continued. "Midori, is it okay if I call you that?"

Midori nodded. "It is my name," he smiled.

"Midori, with all due respect, what are you doing?"

"I need to go to New York. I cannot stay here any longer."

"You won't be staying here," Shields replied, "that's for sure." With that, he shook his head and brought an end to the hearing.

The guard brought Midori back to his cell where Landers waited expectantly.

"Well, how'd it go in there, little man?"

Midori allowed a small smile to crease his lips. "Not too well," he replied. "Not too well."

"What's next for you?"

"I don't know, Robert, what's next for you?"

"Oh, they'll let me out soon. How many times can they keep arresting me for public drunkenness? I don't hurt anyone. Well, except that one time with my wife, but no one else," he smiled.

Midori reached into his left pocket for Thumbprint, but the rock wasn't there. He jumped off his bed and began to fuss around in the sheets.

"Whoa, what's up, little man?" Landers asked.

"Nothing, nothing," Midori replied sheepishly as he felt Thumbprint with his right hand in his other pocket. "I'm fine, sorry."

"My friend," Robert began as he eyed Midori, "you can tell an old drunk like me. What happened in your hearing?"

Midori smiled at Landers and nodded. "I guess I can, Robert, thank you. I told them of my plan to go to New York. They weren't happy."

"What's in New York, little man?

"Everything is in New York, Robert!" Midori replied excitedly. "I am a photographer, Robert. I have not been able to truly work in my profession now for a year and a half. I need to go to New York and try my hand. I want to see how I compare." Midori suddenly became silent and looked down at his worn shoes.

"Hey, are you that good, Midori?" Robert asked him.

Midori smiled, but did not answer.

CHAPTER TWENTY-ONE

Salt Lake City, UT

May 22, 1943

Midori awoke alone in his cell. Landers had been released the day before, and Midori felt oddly at a loss. The big man smelled and snorted through the night. But, he was good-hearted and made Midori smile. Midori wondered if he'd seen the last of his cellmate. Of course, he'd also wondered that every other time Landers had been released.

Shortly before 3:00 PM, the guard came to get Midori to bring him to the visitor's area. June and Asano were there and had brought some fresh fruit. Asano shared some Elms Hotel gossip with Midori, and they all had a laugh, but the visit was truncated when the guard returned and told Midori that the warden needed to see him.

The warden nodded to Midori and motioned to him to sit. Then he leaned across his desk and handed Midori a sheet of paper. Midori quickly scanned the page. The letter read as follows:

U.S. Department of Justice, Immigration and Naturalization Service

MEMORANDUM FOR ALIEN ENEMY INFORMATION BUREAU
OFFICE OF THE PROVOST MARSHALL GENERAL
WAR DEPARTMENT, WASHINGTON, D.C.

In Re: Change of Status
  Detained Enemy Alien

The letter then identified Midori and his current status and continued:

Date of Change of Status: 5/19/43 3:40 P.M.

PRESENT STATUS: Interned at: Ft. Missoula, Mont.

So, that was it. Now Midori knew his fate. He was being sent to an internment camp.

JOHN EDGAR HOOVER
DIRECTOR

CONFIDEN.

CC-28&a

Federal Bureau of Investigation
United States Department of Justice
Washington, D. C.

Date: May 21, 1943

To: Assistant Chief of Staff
G-2
War Department
Washington, D. C.

CONFIDENTIAL
BY SPECIAL MESSENGER

Attention: Colonel L. R. Forney

From: J. Edgar Hoover - Director, Federal Bureau of Investigation

Subject: MIDORI ARTHUR SHIMODA

Reference is made to my letter dated __November 9, 1942__, in which you were advised that on __October 15, 1942__, the Attorney General ordered the __parole__ of __Midori Arthur Shimoda__.

For your information, I have received from the Attorney General a copy of another order dated __May 4, 1943__, directing that __Midori Arthur Shimoda be interned__.

...ification Cancelled by Authority

_____ Date _____

OCT 21 1943

CONFIDEN.

199

PART FOUR

CHAPTER TWENTY-TWO

Fort Missoula, MT

June 6, 1943

Midori leaned against the wooden wall behind his metal cot. He held what passed for stationery against a piece of flimsy cardboard from the top of a box, which was balanced on his knees. He took a deep breath and began to write.

Dear Hede:

I hope that you and George are well. And, of course, everyone else too! How are the girls and Papa? And your dad? How is it in Mapleton this time of year? Are the people being nice to all of you?

The internment camp here in Fort Missoula isn't horrible, but, of course, I'm not allowed to leave. I guess this is a different kind of facility from where Roy is because, although there are lots of other Japanese, maybe between 200 and 500, there are also many Italians, too, maybe 500, and a handful of Germans. I am told that everyone else here is citizens, and most everyone is a lot older than me for they are issei, first generation born in Japan: many have kids my age. I guess where Roy is, most all were born here, nissei, so are official citizens.

How is Roy, have you heard from him? Seems like just another situation where I am in a different place and looked upon differently from most of the rest.

Because there are so many Japanese here, the cooks make rice. Lots of rice! Almost every meal. I hear there were even more Japanese last year, but some have been moved to other camps while others have, apparently, been released. I live in what's called the "Japanese Compound," since we're mostly segregated by race.

I have been keeping busy and staying out of trouble. Anyone has the opportunity to work out in the fields at 10 cents an hour, which is the internationally agreed pay for the prisoners of war. Even so, the set up impresses me as slave labor, so I'm refraining from it. However, I keep myself plenty busy with tennis and baseball. And, I help out in the kitchen. We all have the chance to work in the kitchen or the laundry.

Also, they show us lots of movies. Every Tuesday and Saturday afternoon, it seems. The Italians all shriek and scream every time a pretty actress is on the screen. The guards don't seem to mind.

With love to all,

Midori

Midori re-read the letter, folded it, and placed it in an envelope.

"You know," the man sprawled out on the next cot called over to Midori, "the censors read all of our letters before they go out. Anything you say that is negative will be cut out of that letter."

Midori smiled and looked to his left. The man lounging on the cot was not quite as short as Midori, though still short, just the same. His trademark was the premature gray streaks in his otherwise dark hair. "Thank you, Masao," Midori said, "but how do you know that since you don't see what is delivered to the person you write to?"

"You will see, my friend, it becomes clear. Like you might say, 'the food here is horrible.' Next letter from the person you wrote to would say, 'so, how's the food, anyway?' You can tell that they've messed around with the letter. It's not quite what you wrote."

Midori rubbed his chin and then swung around on his low-slung cot and placed his feet on the floor as he faced Masao. "Do you think they add anything to our letters?" he asked.

"No, I don't," Masao shook his head vigorously, and Midori caught sight of the gray streaks as his fellow internee's hair swung from left to right. "They would have to imitate our handwriting, and I think that's too hard."

Midori nodded his agreement. "Masao, thanks again for explaining everything to me. You are a pro, very experienced at this. You are very helpful to a newcomer like me."

Masao smiled. "We have all been newcomers at one time or another, Midori, so we help each other. I am not doing anything you wouldn't do for me."

"Lights out soon, right, Masao?" Midori asked, sweeping his right arm around to indicate the entire barracks that he and Masao shared with 35 or so other internees.

"Yes, it's actually pretty late; the guards must've forgotten."

◆ ◆ ◆

Midori shivered as he awoke to the sound of Reveille. How cold was it, he wondered? It's June, he thought. Montana is not a place Midori wanted to return to any time soon. He climbed out of bed and pulled on his socks. He quickly pulled on his pants over the long underwear in which he'd slept.

As usual, Masao slept right through Reveille. Midori looked over at his new friend, who though three or four inches taller, probably weighed about the same as Midori. Midori had worried when he first saw Masao that perhaps the food would be rationed, but that wasn't the case. Masao was just waif-like.

The internees were responsible for making and serving the food, and, while not plentiful, it was sufficient. Most breakfasts consisted of fruit and tea or coffee. Some mornings, a new cereal called "Cheeri-oats" was served. Some of the internees thought it a kind of delicacy, but Midori didn't understand the fuss. It tasted dry, and milk only went so far to help improve it.

Midori woke Masao, who ran his hand through his hair, yawned so widely that Midori worried the man's jaw would snap and then popped out of bed. As they left the barracks, Midori followed what had become his new ritual. First, he looked at the guard tower closest to the barracks. It was 40 feet tall and large enough to house five or six men at a time with room left over. The towers were constructed of wood and were accessible by a long wooden staircase. He then traced around the perimeter of the camp using his eyes as his guide. He followed the fence, which was ten feet tall and topped with barbed wire, around to the left until it was interrupted by a ground-level guard tower. He was about to continue along toward the next large guard tower when he sensed Masao eying him, so he turned to face his friend.

"Why do you do that every day, Midori, you trying to plan your escape?"

"No, no, no," Midori laughed. "Not at all. I'm not looking to get in any trouble. Besides, have you seen the way the guards are armed? They have billy clubs, gas masks, and tear gas guns. I bet they can't wait to try to use all of that stuff!"

Masao smiled wryly. "I don't think so. The guards know we aren't going anywhere. They don't want trouble any more than we do."

Midori smiled just slightly. "Okay, that's good. I mean, I've been roughed up a bit in the past but never hit with a billy club. No reason to start now."

Masao snorted. "No offense, my little friend, but the cops or guards usually use billy clubs when they're worried physically and need an edge. Sorry to say, I don't think you exactly strike fear in them," Masao chuckled.

Midori patted his new friend playfully. "You aren't exactly a big weightlifter yourself, Masao. Tell me, were you ever arrested?"

"Does being brought here count? Is that an arrest? If so, then, yes, once. If not, then, well, no."

The two walked along playfully bantering and headed into the mess hall. They sat down at the long wooden table with the other internees, the Japanese sitting at one end of the large hall and the Italians at the other. The room wasn't big enough to seat everyone at once, so there were two seatings for every meal. Midori and Masao chose the first seating when given the chance.

As breakfast ended, Midori headed back toward the kitchen with his and Masao's bowls. One of Midori's jobs at the camp was meal clean up. Just as he was about to enter the kitchen, Midori spied several of the guards striding purposefully into the mess hall. He stopped and watched as they approached Masao and two or three others. Words were exchanged, not angry, but firm. The guards pointed, and the men went off with them. Midori squinted as he tried to decipher Masao's facial expression, but his friend was inscrutable. There was no violence, no raised voices. Still, it was disconcerting to see the men led out by the guards.

Midori pursed his lips, inhaled, and headed for the back of the kitchen. Walking to his usual spot at the sink in the far corner, Midori grabbed a towel and began to dry the bowls that were piling up where they'd been washed by other internees. Midori strained to understand the combination of Portuguese and English being spoken by the small group assigned to dish and bowl clean up. A few were from South America and spoke no English. Some knew a bit of English and some Portuguese, while Midori and others spoke English, but no Portuguese. The internees spoke very little Japanese. Mostly the men just pointed and smiled.

An hour or so later Midori returned to the barracks to tidy up his area. Masao's bed was mildly rumpled, and it was clear he hadn't returned since breakfast. Midori smoothed his friend's bed covers and waited for inspection. The guards weren't particular. As long as the beds were made, and the clothes cubbies neat, they generally overlooked other, minor transgressions.

Today's inspector was John, a small, fastidious, but friendly man with a quick smile. He greeted Midori and seemed not at all bothered by Masao's absence. Before John moved on, Midori spoke.

"Excuse me, so sorry to bother you while you complete inspection, but do you know where Masao went?"

"Probably to a loyalty hearing. Everyone has them. You'll have yours soon enough. They take you into the courtroom," John motioned over his shoulder, "and they press you on who you want to win the war. They try to trip you up, but no one ever seems to fail." John smiled. "He'll be back by later in the day, and he'll be fine."

Midori smiled and nodded. "Thank you, that is very helpful and a relief to know."

Several hours later, Midori was outside talking to several of the other internees when Masao approached them, smiling.

"Masao!" Midori exclaimed as he vigorously patted his friend's shoulder. Is it true what John, the guard, told me that you had a loyalty hearing?"

"Yes, my friend, it's true. I guess that's one thing I haven't told you about yet."

Midori listened with rapt attention as Masao described the loyalty hearing. When Masao finished, he said, "remember what I said about the beginning. They open with the Pledge of Allegiance, and they watch closely to see who is reciting it and how well we know the words."

Midori stood in front of Masao, his hands thrust deep in his pockets. Despite the warm sunshine, Midori shivered whenever he stood in the shade. He absent-mindedly fingered Thumbprint, turning the rock over and over in his pocket as Masao finished entertaining the small group with his story.

Once Masao was done talking, Midori slipped away and headed back toward the main building in the Japanese Compound. He quickly found his way over to the side of the building where the men stored their rocks. At first, Midori had been mystified by all of the beautiful stones until Masao explained it to him. The rocks surfaced when the snows melted each Spring. They were quite attractive right away according, to Masao. Smooth, with pretty lines. The men all took to making them even more beautiful by polishing them in a variety of ways. First, the men would take them to the showers, which had a cement floor, and they'd rub them across the floor for hours. Then, they'd take the government issued blankets and polish some more. The men were making the rocks into jewelry, ashtrays, and other objects and sending them to their loved ones. Midori had smiled broadly, and quickly joined the rock collecting activities the moment he'd learned about them. He had several projects in the process as he found his way to the compound.

PEBBLE ART PRODUCED BY INTERNEES (C. 1943), COURTESY OF
THE HISTORICAL MUSEUM AT FORT MISSOULA.

FT. MISSOULA ROAD THROUGH BARRACKS (C. 1943), COUR-
TESY OF THE HISTORICAL MUSEUM AT FORT MISSOULA.

209

FT. MISSOULA MESS HALL (C. 1943), COURTESY OF THE HIS-
TORICAL MUSEUM AT FORT MISSOULA.

FT. MISSOULA GUARD TOWER (C. 1943), COURTESY OF THE
HISTORICAL MUSEUM AT FORT MISSOULA.

CHAPTER TWENTY-THREE

Fort Missoula, MT

August 31, 1943

"Hey, Shimoda," called out J.P. Wheeler, the lanky guard watching over the men, "how many hours you gonna waste tryin' to teach them Italian guys how to play baseball?" Wheeler spit as he spoke and then quickly placed his foot over his spittle and ground it into the dirt.

"Mr. Wheeler, it is a fun pursuit. They are nice enough, and they are trying. Plus, our team already beat all of the other Japanese teams; we need someone else to play."

"Someone else to beat, you mean, Shimoda!"

Midori persisted with his teaching, demonstrating to his fellow internees how to hold a bat and how to throw a baseball. There were no baseball gloves in the camp, so the games were barehanded affairs, which led to much shaking off of sudden stings when the men tried to catch hard-hit balls. The Italians were good-natured opponents. Still, as neophytes, they were no match for Midori and his teammates, a number of whom had played baseball growing up in California, Oregon, or Washington.

After several short games, it came down to two Japanese teams playing each other while many of the other Japanese and a large number of the Italian men watched and alternately cheered and jeered. The teams were locked in a tense, though good-natured battle when Midori received the proverbial "tap on the shoulder," telling him it was time for his loyalty hearing. Despite Masao's assurances that all would be fine, Midori felt a tiny bit of sweat forming on his brow as he headed with J.P. towards Post Headquarters building, T-1, which was being used as a makeshift courtroom. J.P. was talkative, almost jovial as they walked, but Midori's mind was racing. What would they ask? What should he say?

Midori entered the formidable T-1 for the first time since his internment. The inside took on a dark hue in contrast to the bright sunshine, even though it was reasonably well lit. J.P. brought Midori to a door on the left and opened it to reveal a large room set up for hearings. There were two wooden tables of equal size, perhaps large enough to seat six. Their sturdy legs sat parallel to each other facing the front of the room. Directly in front of them was a stage-like area where, undoubtedly, the hearing examiner would sit, elevated above the rest of the room. On the wall to one side of the hearing examiner's desk was a large photo portrait of President Roosevelt. To the other side was a slightly smaller photo portrait of Cordell Hull, the Secretary of State.

To the left of the tables on the lower level were three rows of folding chairs. J.P. motioned to Midori to sit in one of the chairs next to nine other Japanese internees who were already there.

Midori soaked up his surroundings. He'd seen so many hearing rooms recently, and they all had so many similarities. Wooden tables and chairs. The raised, stage-like area for the examiners to sit. None of it particularly comfortable. As Midori made his mental notes, he was taken by the complete silence of the other internees. After about thirty minutes, warden Don Strickland came in and assumed his place on the stage, looking down imperially at the internees.

"Men," he began, "we are at war with a cowardly enemy. We've been attacked. And, when attacked, we fight back hard, it's the American way! Please all stand, and we will now recite the Pledge of Allegiance."

The men stood as one and, with varying degrees of success, recited the Pledge. Midori made sure to make eye contact with Strickland as he confidently called out the words.

"Okay, men, this is how this goes. You will each be given a loyalty hearing during which I, and I alone, will assess whether you're a loyal resident of this great country or whether we have reason to believe you are trying to deceive us while you work for the enemy. I ask the questions; you answer the questions. Each hearing takes about 10 minutes. Okay, J.P., please take nine of these men across the hall to wait since each hearing is confidential."

Midori was swept up as part of the group of nine sent to wait. The men exchanged some minor conversation but mostly sat in silence as they awaited their turns with Strickland. After three others had been called and completed their hearings, it was Midori's turn. J.P. brought him into the hearing room and introduced him to Strickland, who nodded at Midori to sit down. Strickland shuffled through some papers on the table in front of him as Midori watched him. He was impeccably dressed in khaki pants and a buttoned-down white shirt. His brown shoes shone brightly. One rogue hair kept popping off to the left on his otherwise perfectly combed, short, gray-flecked hair.

Strickland looked up with an expression that wasn't unfriendly but didn't invite small talk either. Midori met his gaze and waited patiently. Finally, Strickland put down the file and spoke.

"Why did you get sent here, Mr. Shimoda? Most of our Japanese internees have been here from the start, but you just got here a few months ago. Why?"

"While at work, I have shared that my goal is to work in New York City among the best photographers in the country, perhaps the world. Well, since I was on parole, I was arrested for saying this. I could not be charged with an offense since I had not committed a crime, so, the US Attorney, Mr. Shields, felt it would be best for me to come here."

"Felt it would be best, how? Did he think you were a threat to the US?"

Midori shuffled his feet just a bit and looked down at his shoes. He knew Strickland had a file loaded with information. Midori didn't want to dispute anything that Shields, Mutz, or anyone else had reported. Still, he didn't want to inflame the situation either.

"I don't know, Mr. Strickland," Midori finally indicated. "I think maybe he thought I was hiding something when I said I needed to go to New York, but I am not hiding anything."

"What will you do in New York, Mr. Shimoda? Got a job? Got a girl?

"No, sir, neither. I will find work as a photography technician. I can retouch photos to make them look much better. People like that."

Strickland leaned back in his chair and smiled. "Can you get this darn gray stuff out if we take a picture," he laughed, running his fingers through his tightly cut hair.

Midori smiled back. "Yes, sir, I bet I could."

"You married Midori?" Strickland asked, his voice now friendly.

"I am separated, soon to be divorced."

"Sorry to hear that. Our government likes internees who are married, Mr. Shimoda. It gives them a reason to stay here and to be loyal."

"Margaret didn't want to be a family woman; Mr. Strickland, it was a hurtful time."

"Fair enough, Mr. Shimoda, we won't speak of it again. So, tell me," Strickland shifted gears, "how do you think things are going with the war effort?"

"Mr. Strickland, we don't get much information in here," Midori smiled, "but from what I hear, the tide is turning in our favor."

"When you say 'our' who do you mean, Mr. Shimoda?"

Midori stood ramrod straight and looked Strickland directly in the eye. "America, Mr. Strickland. This is my country. America."

Strickland smiled. "Mine too, Midori, mine too. J.P. please take Mr. Shimoda on out and bring in the next internee."

CHAPTER TWENTY-FOUR

Fort Missoula, MT

September 15, 1943

"Let's go you two," J.T. called out to Midori and Masao. "We haven't got all day, you know," he smiled.

Midori scampered over to the guard carrying two fishing poles, a bucket, and a small package of bait. Masao had two poles as well, and a pail, but would share the bait Midori carried.

"All ready, you guys, first time out of the camp in a while, right?"

Midori motioned to his friend to respond. Masao spoke up, "I have been here since March of 1942. So, a year and a half. I've never set foot outside this fence."

I also have not set foot outside of the camp, J.T., but, as you both know, I just got here this past May, so it's just a few months," Midori explained.

"Okay, not sure what came over Strickland, but he told me I could take a couple of internees on this fishing trip. Of course, we're going to catch fish for Strickland and his family to eat, so maybe it's a statement about my lousy fishing more than about Strickland loosening the reins," the young guard laughed.

"Whatever the reason, we are grateful," Masao offered, smiling broadly.

"Yes," Midori replied. "Grateful."

"You guys are my two model prisoners. Now, no funny business out there, you two, you hear?" J.T. allowed just a touch of sternness to creep into his boyish voice.

Midori and Masao both nodded vigorously in tandem. J.T. laughed and said, "that's what I'm talking about! Okay, we need to grab Murph at the east guard tower on the way out, he's joining us."

The banks of the Bitterroot River weren't far and the four walked there quickly. Midori and Masao in front, and Murph and J. T. behind them. To an outsider at another time, they could have appeared to be four friends going fishing. But, nothing could be further from the truth as the internees led the way so the guards could watch them.

The river glimmered with sunshine. Crystal clear water lapped the shore where the men set up their rods. Midori touched the water and briefly recoiled at the cold temperature. It was very late in the summer, and evening temperatures routinely dropped into the forties, making it tough for the water to stay warm. Midori stood and took in the water, the branches hanging over it from the shore and the deep blue sky.

The fishing wasn't bad. Not amazing, but not bad. Midori and Masao kept up their end and caught every bit as many trout as the more experienced guards. Before long, the quartet had more than enough trout for Strickland and his family—both buckets were filled—and they headed back to camp.

Even the partial freedom was intoxicating to Midori and Masao. They sauntered on the way back, not wanting to pass through the gate, not wanting to see the barbed wire and the guard towers. But, it wasn't that long a walk, and soon enough they passed from freedom to captivity. Other internees looked on with a mixture of surprise and envy as they saw Midori and Masao walking with the guards, carrying the poles and buckets of fish.

"Strickland will be happy," J.T. offered, just as a short, tightly muscled guard named White came running up.

"What is it, White?" J.T. asked, "what's so dad blamed important, that you're running over here so out of breath?"

White looked at J.T. for a moment, but then addressed Midori. "Mr. Strickland has been looking for you for about an hour. You'd better get over there."

Midori glanced at his fishing buddies. "Thanks for a great day," he said softly. "I must go and find out what this is about."

White hustled Midori along quickly toward Strickland's office. Although he was curious, Midori couldn't take White as seriously as White took himself. Midori tried to keep up but fell behind enough that White turned around and motioned for him to move faster. Midori began to trot to keep up until they reached the entrance to Strickland's office, where White led him in.

"Have a seat, Mr. Shimoda," Strickland said, his face revealing nothing as he indicated the lone chair across from his desk. Midori quickly noticed that the surface was immaculate; a few files in the left-hand corner, a cup of pens on the right. "That is all, thank you, Mr. White," Strickland continued motioning the guard out. Midori glanced at White, who looked very disappointed to be relieved of his duties.

"Mr. Shimoda, after we had your loyalty hearing, I looked into your case a bit more deeply. You seem to me to be a very bright man, Mr. Shimoda."

"Thank you, sir," Midori replied.

"And, frankly. . . now don't take this the wrong way, you are about the last person I'd fear if I saw you on the street."

Midori smiled but said nothing.

"Now, of course, physical strength isn't necessary to spy for the enemy, only a determination to hurt our country. But, you know what Mr. Shimoda?"

"Sir?"

"Of all of the loyalty hearings I held, yours was the one that stuck with me. I asked myself, 'what is he doing here?'" And, you know what I think, Mr. Shimoda?

"No, sir, I don't."

"I think you are here because of a mistake, Mr. Shimoda. Now, maybe it was your mistake. Maybe Mr. Mutz and Mr. Shields contributed to it, I don't know for sure. But, it was a mistake in the final analysis. I don't think you belong here, Mr. Shimoda."

Midori smiled. "Sir, if I may say so, that's the first time I've ever been happy to have someone tell me that I don't belong!"

Strickland broke out into a huge grin. "That's undoubtedly true, Mr. Shimoda! I'm going to miss you, even though we barely got to know each other. J.T. tells me that you are a model internee and that you have set a high bar for the others. Not the kind of person we want to let leave, actually," Strickland continued, a twinkle evident in his eye.

Midori stood and held Strickland's gaze. "Sir," he began, "I am happy that you have heard well of me. I have tried very hard to do the right thing here. I want nothing more than to contribute to the end of this war for America. We must all see the defeat of the terrible enemy."

Strickland stood and thrust out his hand. "Mr. Shimoda," he said, "we are paroling you, effective tomorrow. You will have your meals with us tonight and in the morning and then we will have a car waiting for you outside the east gate to take you to the train station. After that, you are on your own."

Midori hustled back to the dorm to find Masao and share the good news. Before he located his friend, he noticed a letter on his bed. He opened it and read:

Dear Midori:

So good to hear from you again. We are well, but very worried about you and, of course, about Roy and his family. Roy isn't much for writing, but the last letter from his wife, Tsuru, indicated that the children were not doing well. They are very scared and don't understand why they are being held captive. It helps that they are with their parents, of course, but they are still nervous, according to Tsuru.

Our girls miss you very much. And, of course, your dad, and George and me. We all miss you. When do you think you might be released, any idea? You know, you always have a home with us.

All my love,

Hede

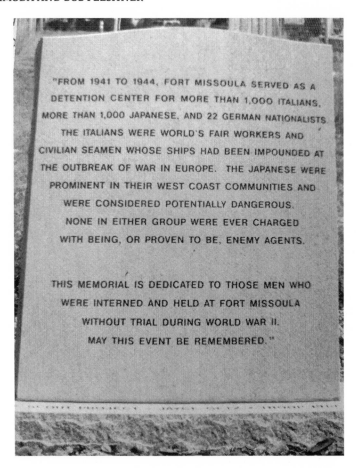

FT. MISSOULA MONUMENT TO DETAINEES

CHAPTER TWENTY-FIVE

Salt Lake City, UT

September 20, 1943

Midori put his small suitcase on the sidewalk and looked up at the house his older brother, George, shared with his wife, Hede, and their daughters May, Janet, and Donna. It had been just over 18 months since Midori had been with May on their trip from Pasadena to Monticello, Utah, before George came to retrieve her and bring her to Mapleton.

Papa will be here too, Midori thought as he took it all in before picking up his suitcase and heading toward the front door. Midori noticed that a bit of the pale yellow paint was peeling, and panes were missing in one of the upstairs windows. Still, the house looked peaceful in the afternoon sun.

Before Midori could knock, he heard a squeal and May came charging through the open door to hug him. Her sisters and George quickly followed her. Hede stood smiling in the doorway with her own slightly stooped father, Terazawa, on one side of her, and Papa Shimoda on the other. Midori noticed that Hede's smile was as luminous as ever, and her long black hair still a defining feature. The elderly men on either side of her seemed to bask in her aura, as they tried desperately to stand up straight, their spines only partially permitting them.

Midori took turns hugging and shaking hands all around. George grabbed the suitcase and mussed Midori's hair, which made all the girls laugh. Before long, they were in the small house exchanging stories.

"Okay," Midori eventually said, "enough about me. Please tell me about you, and all of our brothers and sister, where are they?"

George took a deep breath. Midori could see gray along George's temples that he didn't remember from mere months ago. "You know, of course, that Sets got married. Hede wrote to you about that. To Frank, I think you may have met him."

Midori nodded. "I bet she looked like a princess at the wedding," he smiled.

"She always looks like a princess, Midori-san," George said, smiling as broadly as his younger brother. "As Hede wrote to you, Roy, his wife, Tsuru, and their girls, Carol and Sally, are in a camp. Heart Mountain Camp in Wyoming. There's been some trouble there," George clucked, "but they have steered clear of it."

"What kind of trouble?" Midori inquired, his eyes narrowing.

"They tried to draft Nisei into the service, but some refused and said, 'we will only go fight when we are free.' Others were drafted, but Roy was too old. Tsuru writes when she can and she makes it sound okay, but, like Hede wrote, the girls are scared. Mostly, it sounds like the way you described Ft. Missoula, to be honest. They are imprisoned and cannot leave, but they are well fed and have beds. Maybe you should tell them your secret so they can get released too," George smiled.

"And, Jack and K.G.?"

"Jack still lives in Michigan. He wasn't affected by any of this war stuff as best we can tell and in fact is running a restaurant across the street from a munitions' factory! We only hear from him occasionally. And K.G. is in Iowa. He went to school there to become an osteopathic doctor, as you know, and was smart enough not to come back. We hear from him from time to time, but not too much."

The family briefing continued over dinner. Midori enjoyed his first home-cooked dinner as a free man in months as Hede made fish with pickled vegetables. George and Hede began to discuss sleeping arrangements when Midori cut them off.

"Brother, you are so very kind to have me stay here. I am happy to sleep on the couch or even the floor. Just to know that I can come and go as I please is enough for me right now."

"Midori, the girls want to have a big sleepover in one room in one bed. They will give you a bed that we can bring into Dad's room," Hede explained.

After a bit of bed shuffling, followed by much excitement among the girls at the thought of all sleeping in one bed, it was settled. Midori was happy to share a room with Papa, and the two spoke softly on into the night.

The next day Midori was up early, and he watched the sunrise from the back porch. He looked at the houses across the back alley, some of which had fallen into slight disrepair, others of which appeared in far better shape. He stood and walked around the front toward the sidewalk to glance back at the house and the broken panes of glass.

Midori felt for his wallet but knew how much was in there without checking. He'd been given $25 by Strickland when he left but had to use a portion of it for the train and bus rides back. Still, he'd stashed away over $100 in a hidden compartment of his wallet. And, there was the money he'd left with his former roommate, George.

The morning passed with Midori helping his brother, George, at the produce stand that George co-managed a few blocks from the house. The girls were in school, and Hede stayed home with Papa Shimoda and her father, Terazawa-san. Both were moving slowly at this point and welcomed Hede's company. Her offering of help was always low-key and never obvious. Hede was deceptively strong and moved with the ease of someone half her age. Midori could quickly see how much the men both relied upon and adored her.

Once he finished at the produce stand, Midori cleaned up and headed for Stokes Photography Studio. As he walked through the door, G.B. Stokes screamed out, "Midori's back! They let him out!"

The men shared handshakes and hugs. Midori met Steven, the tall, prematurely balding, young man who had taken Midori's place after his arrest. Steven smiled, shook Midori's hand, and then headed off to help a customer who had just come into the shop. Richard Stokes motioned to Midori to follow him, and the two went to the back of the store.

"Midori, you were one of the finest employees we ever had. I'm sorry it ended the way it did," Midori's former boss declared.

"I understand, Richard. I blame no one. I was very excited about going to New York, and I think that Mr. Mutz and Mr. Shields thought I must be up to no good."

"What will you do now?" Stoked inquired.

Midori tried to suppress an impish grin as he replied, "I plan to go to New York."

Stokes stood ramrod straight and held Midori's gaze. "Seriously?" he asked.

"Seriously," Midori replied evenly.

"So, here we go again?"

"No, not 'here we go again.' I will get permission to go this time. I have a meeting tomorrow with Mr. Sullivan, the immigration officer for Salt Lake City. I am required to check in with him just like I had to with Mr. Mutz before I was interned. I will not leave Salt Lake until I have permission, I promise."

"Okay, that's a relief, Midori. We don't want to have to be involved in any of this, to be honest. Now," and here, Stokes looked down and studied his feet, "I wish we could offer you your job back, but we have young Steven out there now. He's no Midori, but he's competent, and the customers seem to like him well enough."

Midori waved off Richard. "I completely understand," he indicated. "Besides, I didn't come here to ask you to re-hire me; I came only to say 'hello.' I am going to be leaving for New York before long, anyway," he smiled.

CHAPTER TWENTY-SIX

Salt Lake City, UT

September 21, 1943

The second to last Tuesday in September was also the start of Fall, and it felt like it to Del Sullivan. The Officer in Charge of the Salt Lake City division of the Immigration and Naturalization service sat at his desk and shivered. He took turns buttoning and unbuttoning his gray suit jacket as his need for warmth battled his need for comfort, his belly bulging against both his pants and his jacket. His worn brown belt was tethered via the very last hole, so Sullivan found no refuge there. He tried to inhale his way to comfort, but finally gave up and opened the file folder on his overmatched desk.

Sullivan had read the letter from US Attorney Dan Shields at least a half dozen times. The timing of it was entirely out of whack. Sullivan had tried to reach both Edward Ennis, to whom the letter was addressed and Shields himself, both to no avail. So, he was on his own as his meeting with an enemy alien, Midori Shimoda, approached. Still pondering the issue, Sullivan took out the letter and scanned it again.

The letter was dated September 1, 1943 and addressed to Edward Ennis in his capacity as the Director of the Alien Enemy Control Unit with the Department of Justice in Washington, DC. Its author, Dan Shields, was the US Attorney for Salt Lake City. Shields had been in charge of the Shimoda case since day one, that much was clear to Sullivan. What was less clear was how it was that Shimoda would be coming in for a meeting in under an hour as a man paroled from Ft. Missoula. Sullivan re-read the letter yet again:

Dear Mr. Ennis:

I am advised by the Immigration and Naturalization Service representatives here that under an order of the Attorney General dated August 23, 1943, continuing in full force and effect, a previous order of parole dated May 4, 1943 concerning the above-named alien, who is presently detained at Missoula, Montana, has been vacated. I am further advised that this young man has been given interim parole and this parole has been made dependent upon approval or disapproval by me. I think that I should disapprove this interim parole and am accordingly reporting to you the reason for this position.

This young man came to Utah at the time of the evacuation from California. He is a photographer by trade and an alien by birth. He apparently has had a good deal of educational opportunity and speaks the English language with real ease. When he came to Utah he did a peculiar thing to begin with. He left the rather populous portion of the state and went down into the southeast corner to the town of Monticello, where he was the only Japanese and there engaged in his photographic operations. He had been there but a short time when he succeeded in making trouble for himself and he then moved from Monticello and went to Blanding, where he lived for a while, doing photographic work. He engratiated (sic) himself with some of the citizens there and appeared to be getting along all right, but an adverse report was made to the Federal Bureau of Investigation and that organization investigated him and he was arrested and brought to Salt Lake for hearing. The Enemy Alien Hearing Board heard his case and gave subject a chance to fully state his history, which he did in some detail. As the result of that hearing, he was paroled and was given opportunity for employment here in Salt Lake, which seemed to be very satisfactory to him. He was working for a photographer and continued in that line of work for five months. One day, with no apparent reason, Shimoda appeared before Inspector Mutz of the Immigration Bureau and told him that he had decided to quit his job and leave Salt Lake and that he was going to New York and that it didn't make any difference whether we would allow him to go or not, that he had determined to go and that he was impelled to take this step as the result of a confidential arrangement which he had, and even though he knew that the result to him might be disastrous, he was going to go, with or without authority. Mr. Mutz tried to get a statement from alien as to what had determined him on this adventure and here he refused to talk and said that he planned to commit some act after leaving here, either with or without authority, which would eventually result in his internment. He was examined and re-examined upon the point and given an opportunity to be frank about what was worrying him. We could get absolutely nothing from him and so I concluded that a young man as bright as this alien was and as thoroughly equipped, might be dangerous running loose. Accordingly, I agreed with Mr. Mutz that he should be detained until our Enemy Alien Board could work on him. In the meantime an order came from Washington for interment at Missoula, Montana, so the hearing was never had.

As the result of my contacts with this man, I am convinced that he has a plan in mind to do something which may be harmful to the country or the people in it and have been thoroughly satisfied to have him interned, and for that reason I do not believe that he should be allowed on his own until we know more about what was impelling his wilful (sic) violation of orders and his determination to violate them, unless he was restrained. For that reason, I am not in agreement with the parole order which has been recently made.

Very truly yours,

Dan B. Shields
        United States Attorney

Sullivan cracked his knuckles and then put his hands behind his head interlacing his fingers. Lousy timing that Shields was out of town this week, he thought. How in the world did this guy get paroled with a letter like this sitting in the file?

A short time later, Sullivan greeted Midori in the anteroom. "Please, come in," Sullivan motioned to Midori. "Would you like some water?"

Midori declined his questioner's offer and took a seat in the metal folding chair opposite Sullivan's desk. The hearing officer dwarfed his surroundings and took up more than the entire chair as he faced Midori. Though enormous, his presence hewed closer to oafish than to intimidating. Midori noticed that one button on Sullivan's shirt collar was buttoned, the other missing entirely. His tie was knotted, though it sat nowhere near his neck. Midori folded his hands on his lap and waited.

"Mr. Shimoda, you were recently paroled from Ft. Missoula, is that right?"

"Yes, sir, it is." Midori nodded.

"Shouldn't have been, by rights," Sullivan replied.

Midori bit his lip, his stomach twisting, but he did not respond.

I've got a letter here from US Attorney Dan Shields, you know him?"

Midori nodded.

"Well, Mr. Shields was asked to give an opinion about your interim parole, and he said he opposed it," Sullivan explained as he waved the letter from Shields in front of him. "Now, I've been trying to reach Mr. Shields, but, apparently, he got called back to Washington for some big meeting of all the US Attorneys. So, he won't be back for over a week from now.

"I don't know what to do with you, Mr. Shimoda," Sullivan admitted. "I have half a mind to send you back to Ft. Missoula. That'd be my safest course of action. I could also just have you put in jail here in Salt Lake. You know, for safekeeping."

Midori shuffled his feet and looked up. Sullivan's face betrayed confusion, so Midori spoke. "Mr. Sullivan, I can understand your uncertainty given what you say Mr. Shields has written, but I was paroled by Mr. Strickland, the man in charge of Ft. Missoula. He found no reason to hold me. And, with all due respect, sir, I've done nothing since I got back to Salt Lake to warrant you jailing me again. There must be another way to address the situation."

"Situation?" Sullivan said, his voice rising as the word escaped his lips. "Yes," he said, more calmly, "I guess this is just that. A situation." Sullivan mopped his brow with the sleeve of his suit jacket and sat forward in his chair, causing Midori to lean back in his chair.

"Okay," Sullivan finally nodded. "This is what we're gonna do. We're going to recommend that you have a hearing with Mr. Shields to see what he wants to happen now that you're out on parole. In the meantime, I am going to check in with the FBI to see if they think you should go back to jail pending that meeting. I don't need this stress, Mr. Shimoda. I'm going to let you go now, but you need to report to me next Monday and every Monday after that, at least until we set up the meeting with Dan. I mean, Mr. Shields. Is that clear?"

"Yes, Mr. Sullivan. I will be here next Monday, I promise," Midori replied, placing his trembling hands under his legs in a vain attempt to still them.

Midori left Sullivan's office with his stomach performing somersaults as his euphoria at having been paroled was now replaced by a cloud of gloom. The Shields' letter was a shock to Midori, who shook his head as he walked from the office.

Midori strode down the street to get away from Sullivan's office as quickly as he could. He slowed as he got closer to the business district, but he passed shop window after shop window without noticing even one display. Midori didn't know how long he'd been walking when he found himself staring up at the front door to the Elms Hotel. His mood brightened at the sight of the wide stairway leading up. He pulled back his shoulders, breathed deeply, and headed up the stairs. He entered the building and saw the old, familiar hallway, which still smelled faintly of cleaning fluid. He bounded up the staircase to the second floor and then slowed to a walk.

Midori approached his former residence with some mild trepidation. He knocked on the door, but there was no answer. He eventually gave up and shuffled across the hall to the Yamashitas. Susie and Sab would be in school, given that it was early afternoon. Maybe June, too. Perhaps Asano was home, though. Midori tapped lightly on the door. No response. He waited a few minutes and then slowly made his way down the wide staircase and out the front door.

Midori wandered streets he'd covered many times before. He felt forlorn after his lonely visit to the Elms. It was a sign, Midori thought. It was time to leave Salt Lake.

CHAPTER TWENTY-SEVEN

Salt Lake City, UT

October 4, 1943

Midori had laid out a shirt and a pair of pants the night before in hopes that the wrinkles would somehow magically disappear in time for his meeting with U.S. Attorney Dan Shields. He'd partially succeeded. He ate a couple of pieces of fruit from the bowl on the kitchen table, reminded George about his appointment, and headed out well before the appointed time.

Over the past few weeks, Midori had taken to walking for hours around Salt Lake City. He had two or three favorite routes that took him past some beautiful flower gardens in the best residential neighborhoods in the city. While he felt the occasional harsh look from a resident or two, more often than not, Midori was met with a nod or a slight smile from those he passed on the streets. One gentleman occasionally engaged him in discussions about his vegetable garden.

Eventually, Midori found his way to US Attorney Dan Shields' office. He strode purposefully up the marble stairs and through the imposing wood door. A secretary greeted Midori and asked him to wait in the room adjacent to the hearing room. Midori complied, wondering if he was about to face another full-blown hearing or if this would be something different.

Within a few minutes, Dan Shields walked into the room and stuck out his hand. "Good morning, Mr. Shimoda," he said as they greeted each other. "Please follow me; we're just going to meet in my office today."

Shields had a strong stride, and, at nearly a foot taller than Midori, he took two steps for every three of Midori's. Midori smiled inwardly. Trotting to keep up was a daily occurrence.

"Have a seat, Mr. Shimoda," Shields' requested with a sweep of his arm. His office was well appointed, with comfortable, cloth-covered, beige armchairs sitting on either side of a low-slung coffee table. Shields snapped a file from his desk and joined Midori on the other side of the room. They sat in the arm-chairs facing each other, and Midori waited, his lower lip curling slightly in anticipation.

"Mr. Shimoda," the U.S. Attorney began, "our paths seem to keep crossing." Shields' voice was calm, his manner friendly. Midori thought that, if anything, Shields had even less hair than the last time they met. His blue eyes were still memorable, though perhaps a touch less piercing than during the previous meeting.

"Yes, sir, it seems that way," Midori replied evenly.

"I'm not sure how you were paroled, Mr. Shimoda. Mr. Sullivan told me that he has explained the situation to you. I wrote to Mr. Ennis and strongly urged them to keep you interned, are you aware of that?"

Midori nodded. "Mr. Sullivan told me when we met, that was the first I'd heard of it."

"My understanding from Mr. Sullivan," Shields continued, "is that my letter somehow never made it to Mr. Strickland, who arranged for your parole from Ft. Missoula. Sometimes we are not that efficient, Mr. Shimoda, but I'd rather we be inefficient in things that don't relate to our national security."

Midori caught Shields' gaze and held it, though not in a negative or threatening way. As Shields began to avert his eyes, Midori spoke. "Mr. Shields, I am very sorry that you think I might be a risk to the national security of this country. I understand that it's your job to look for risks, but, with all due respect, I am not one, sir."

Shields nodded. "I certainly thought that until your last hearing, Mr. Shimoda. But, you were so darn adamant about going to New York and doing something that would get you interned, that I started to doubt my initial beliefs about you. And, if I have any doubt, ever, about someone, I need to get them in jail or an internment camp.

"All of that being said, I am willing to give you another chance. Do you want to explain yourself from that last hearing? Maybe tell me about New York or whatever else was bothering you so much? You seemed very agitated."

Midori sat up straight in his chair and placed his right arm on the armrest. "Mr. Shields," he began in a soft, though firm voice. "I am sorry if I have caused trouble or doubt for you. I must go to New York for professional reasons. I have not had much chance at all to work in my chosen profession of photography for over one and a half years. New York is the best place in America for me to try my hand at top end professional photography. I must search for my own, personal Shinjitsu. My truth."

Shields leaned back and nodded as he appraised Midori. "What do you take pictures of, Mr. Shimoda?"

"Many things. I was a yearbook and event photographer back in California. I've taken many, many photos of models. I also photograph food and other products. I also like to find beauty in the elements of nature. A few works I am proud of feature a disassembled raw onion on a sheet of glass and the long afternoon shadow cast by a lawn rake propped against the side of a building. I also love the desert."

Shields nodded. "But, last time we checked, you didn't have a job. Or a place to live in New York. Is that still the case? Oh, and, to be perfectly blunt, we don't want you taking pictures."

"Yes, sir, I understand, I will get work quickly. I will go out as soon as I get there and apply for work re-touching photos, working on developing, tinting, and other dark room type tasks that many photographers don't like to do. I will find the busiest studios where the owners don't have time for those things. I will do them," Midori continued, his voice quickening with excitement. "And, then, at some point, after the war ends, I will have an opportunity to take pictures and to match myself against the very best," he finished with a flourish.

Shields took his time looking at the folder. "Okay, fine on that, but what else was bothering you, Mr. Shimoda? When we asked about your marriage, you got very excited, almost combative."

Midori breathed deeply and began. "My marriage is a source of great disappointment to me, Mr. Shields. I guess it should never have happened."

Shields rubbed his hands together and bit his upper lip under his lower one. Suddenly, he stood and towered over Midori. He pressed his right foot into the ground and grimaced. "Sorry," he said, "I've got a leg cramp. Must be from my workout this morning. Anyway, I've heard enough. Please let yourself out," he continued as he leaned over and rubbed his calf. "We'll be in touch within a month or so."

CHAPTER TWENTY-EIGHT

Salt Lake City, UT

November 3-18, 1943

TELEGRAM SPECIAL

SALT LAKE CITY UTAH NOV 3 1943 120P

ALIEN ENEMY CONTROL UNIT
ATTN EDWARD J ENNIS

RE 146-13-2-77-254 MIDORI ARTHUR SHIMODA THIS MAN ASKS AUTHORITY TO GO TO NEW YORK AND HIS REQUEST DISAPPROVED BY IMMIGRATION SERVICE BELIEVE IF SERVICE WERE TOLD SOMETHING OF THE MAN HIS REQUEST WOULD BE GRANTED MATTER HANGING FOR THIRTY DAYSAND WE BE-LIEVE REQUEST SHOULD BE GRANTED CAN YOU DO ANYTHING ABOUT IT

DAN B SHIELDS US ATTY.

◆ ◆ ◆

November 8, 1943

Officer in Charge
Immigration and Naturalization Service
Salt Lake City, Utah

In re. MIDORI ARTHUR SHIMODA
Your file 554/A-272

    Requested change in place of parole by the above-named alien enemy will not be approved pending further investigations.

    Please obtain from him a detailed statement as to whether he has definite employment arranged for and the exact type of work he intends to do. It should of course be borne in mind that special permission would have to be obtained from the United States Attorney before he would be authorized to use any type of camera and it is extremely doubtful that authorization would be given for any portable types.

    Your report should also show present employment of this alien and contain your recommendation as to whether it appears practicable to authorize his change in place of residence.

    W. F. Kelly
    Assistant Commissioner

For Alien Control

CC - District Director
    San Francisco, California

CC – DIRECTOR, ALIEN ENEMY CONTROL UNIT – D. J. File:
146-13-2-77-254

Further report will be submitted prior to final decision as to whether change in place of parole will be authorized.

◆ ◆ ◆

3730 S. 9ᵗʰ East
Salt Lake City, Utah
November 16, 1943

Mr. Del L. Sullivan
Officer in Charge
Immigration and Naturalization Service
407 Postoffice (sic) Building
Salt Lake City, Utah

Dear Sir:

It has been requested that I made (sic) a detailed statement as to whether I have employment arranged for in New York City and the exact type of work I intend to enter into.

Being unknown in New York City I have made no definite arrangements for employment. However, I have been recognized as one of the best in my line of work and I feel certain that I will encounter no difficulty in obtaining employment.

As regards the type of work I expect to do I will say that I desire to become connected with the technical or finishing department of some photographic studio. I do not expect to use cameras at all and have had no intention of requesting permission from the United States Attorney to use same. The work I expect to enter into will be similar to that I was doing while on parole in this city. The United States Attorney told me that no special authorization was necessary for that class of work.

I am not employed at present as I have been awaiting a decision in my request for change of parole and residence.

Respectfully,

Midori Shimoda

◆ ◆ ◆

U.S. DEPARTMENT OF JUSTICE
IMMIGRATION AND NATURALIZATION SERVICE
Salt Lake City, Utah

November 16, 1943

Commissioner

Immigration and Naturalization Service

Philadelphia, Pennsylvania

(DIRECT TO EXPEDITE)

Attention: Assistant Commissioner for Alien Control

Your 39/9401; November 8, 1943; MIDORI ARTHUR SHIMODA

There is forwarded letter from subject stating his plans with regard to employment in New York.

It will be noted that he has made no definite arrangements for employment. He is recognized as a very skilled technician in the photographic field, particularly in finishing, developing, tinting, etc., and is a good freehand crayon artist. It appears that he will have no difficulty in securing employment in New York City in a photographic studio or as a commericial (sic) artist.

The subject has been reluctant to associate with Japanese persons, both alien and citizen here, and has incurred enmity of some of them, much of it due, it is believed, to domestic difficulty which he *has had.*

Subject has not been employed since his release from internment. Prior thereto, he was last employed by the Stokes Studio here. No reason is seen why he should not be permitted to change his residence and parole to New York City, and it is recommended that his application be granted.

> *I.F. Wixon*
> *District Director*
> *San Francisco*
> *District*

> *By: Del L. Sullivan*
> *Officer in Charge*
> *Salt Lake City*
> *Office*

◆ ◆ ◆

November 18, 1943

Honorable James B. M. McNally
United States Attorney
New York, New York

Dear Sir:

<u>*Attention Mr. Harold McKee*</u>

United States Attorney Dan B. Shields, Salt Lake City, Utah, has referred to my attention the application of Midori Arthur Shimoda for permission to travel to and reside in New York City.

This alien is presently under parole by order of the Attorney General. His record does not disclose any fact leading to the suspicion that he would be dangerous if residing in New York. In view of his record I do not see any objection to his change of residence to New York City, since he would be under proper supervision by the Immigration and Naturalization Service. The Service, however, indicates that your office objects to the issuance of a travel authorization by Mr. Shields to this alien.

I would appreciate your reconsideration of this request that Mr. Shimoda reside in New York City in the hope that a travel authorization can be issued to him by Mr. Shields, who has telegraphed that "We believe request should be granted. Can you do anything about it?"

If your reconsideration permits the residence of Mr. Shimoda in New York City, will you please advise Mr. Shields at Salt Lake City by telegram.

Very truly yours,

Edward J. Ennis
Director

CHAPTER TWENTY-NINE

Salt Lake City, UT

December 1, 1943

"Christmas in New York, Midori, eh?" George smiled.

"Yes, though I can still hardly believe it!"

"How's the packing going, young man?"

"I have so little, George, I can fit it all in these two small duffle bags. And, no cameras or equipment at all, so not much to carry. I've got some money, so I will buy a coat and some warm clothes when I get to New York. By the way, did you say that June Yamashita is going to meet us at the train station?"

Yes, she wants to say goodbye and good luck. I told her we'd try to get there in time to have a cup of tea with her, so we should go say goodbye to Hede and the others."

Midori picked up his duffles and headed for the front of the house. It was a cool, sunny morning though the house was warm from the many people it held. Midori looked around at the faces of those he loved. He tried to speak, but his words got caught in his throat. Finally, he began moving toward his father.

"Papa, I love you," he began. "I have so much enjoyed these months with you. We will see each other soon," he continued, though he knew that not to be true. The two men hugged for the last time before Midori moved on to his left to face Hede's father, Terazawa-san.

"Good luck, Midori-san," Terazawa-san began. "You come from a fine family, and you will make us all very proud, I am sure."

Midori hugged Terazawa-san for a moment and then let go. "Kind, sir," he said, "getting to know you these months has been one of the pleasures of my life." Midori took the old man's hands and said, "thank you."

Next, it was time for a group hug with the three girls. Then, Midori turned to Hede.

"From the first time I saw you with George those many years ago in Pasadena, I thought you were perfect for him. But, I was wrong, and too limited in my thoughts. You aren't just perfect for George, Hede, you are just perfect." Hede cried as she held onto her brother-in-law.

"You are going to do so well in New York, Midori-san. We will continue to be letter writing partners, okay?' Hede sniffled.

With that, George swept up Midori's duffle bags, and the two were off to the train station.

June was sitting at a table near the front of the station, drinking tea when Midori and George walked in. Her jet-black hair was perfectly brushed and fell the length of her back. She stood and Midori took both of her small hands in his. "So very nice to see you, June! Thank you for coming to the station."

June's smile was luminescent. "I am happy to see you, Midori," she began. "I bring greetings from the entire family. Mama says to stay warm, Susie says to get a record player and always listen to "The Donkey Serenade," and little Sab, well, I can't quite figure out what Sab was saying, but we'll just say that he said, 'good luck,'" she laughed.

George watched with bemusement as his little brother and June exchanged stories of the Elms Hotel. Then, checking his watch, George said, "it's almost time to board. Just one more thing, little brother."

"Yes?" Midori replied, his eyebrows rising with expectation.

George stood and took off his beautiful, custom made navy, wool overcoat. "I know this will be a bit too big for you, but it's going to be cold in New York, so please take this to remember me by."

Midori stood, completely and utterly speechless. He took the coat from George and immediately put it on. It was too big, but not comically so. Midori gathered himself and faced his brother. "I will always remember you, George, even without the coat. You are a wonderful brother from whom I've learned so much. I will miss you more than I can say. Thank you for this amazing gift."

CHAPTER THIRTY

New York City, New York

December 6, 1943

Midori exited the YMCA that was his current, though he hoped temporary, home, and noticed for the first time that morning that it was snowing. He pulled his splendid overcoat tightly across his chest and smiled. Snow fell steadily. Midori watched the flakes hitting a maroon sedan parked on 63rd Street just shy of the corner of Central Park West. Why, he wondered, did some of the flakes stick to the hood of the car while others slithered down and onto the ground? Midori made a mental note to try to learn the answer as he turned and headed west on 63rd Street away from the park.

The meeting with his new parole officer was on Columbus Ave., just a few blocks from the Y. Midori stopped into a Schrafft's for a cup of coffee and quickly headed out so that he was standing in the lobby ten minutes early for his appointment. He thought about the date--almost two years to the day since Pearl Harbor. Midori shook his head and was still thinking about the passage of time when the door to the office in front of him swung open.

"Good morning, Mr. Shimoda, come on in, I'm George German. I'm in charge of the Alien Parole Section."

Midori shook hands with his new parole officer and wondered to himself if he was the only one who found irony in the man's last name.

"I've read through your file, Mr. Shimoda. I see you've been trying to get to New York for more than a little bit of time. What's the reason for that?"

"Mr. German, I am in the field of photography. I do much of the mechanical work related to film development: Re-touching, silhouetting, tinting, things like that. New York has way more commercial photography than anyplace else in the country. Probably anyplace else in the world," Midori smiled.

"You have a job, then?"

"I just arrived two days ago, so, no, not yet. But I will get one immediately!"

German picked at a sesame seed in his front teeth and then grabbed his tie and gave it a slight tug. "As you know, Mr. Shimoda, there's a war going on," he indicated with a wry grin. "Most of the able-bodied men between, oh, about 18 and 28, are gone. Lots of job openings. I expect you back here in two weeks with news that you have a job, is that clear?"

"Yes, sir, I will have work when I see you next."

"Where are you staying, Mr. Shimoda?"

"The YMCA on 63rd street for now. I hope to find other housing once I have a job."

German pushed back from his chair and tugged on his tie again. As he stood, Midori noticed a two or three-inch coffee splotch on the bottom of his pale blue shirt.

"Stay warm, Mr. Shimoda, I'll see you in two weeks," German said, not unkindly.

Midori headed back outside into the snow. He glanced up at the buildings, the likes of which he'd only read about. He marveled at their height as he studied the varied designs. Some looked downright boring to Midori, while others held fascinating detail in their facades. Midori often stopped to take a closer look, squinting to keep the snow at bay.

When he reached the bustling 57th Street, Midori turned left and headed east. He crossed over to the south side of the street as Carnegie Hall came into view. Midori studied the intricate detail of the building. He marveled at the stone masonry and smiled at the people hustling in and out of the building. So many people all striding so purposefully, Midori thought, trying not to grin too much lest he look like the newcomer he was.

As he walked down 57th Street, Midori noticed a small storefront photography studio named Albrecht's. He stepped in from the snow and cold and removed his scarf, careful to knock off the snow while he was still outside.

A woman who was the same height as Midori approached him. She had sandy brown hair pulled back in a severe bun, and she wore boots even though she was inside. A pair of narrow, silver glasses rested upon her head.

"Good morning, may I help you?" she asked Midori.

"Yes, ma'am, thank you," Midori replied, nodding slightly. "I, I am afraid I'm not a customer."

The woman raised her left eyebrow and held Midori's gaze.

"I am a photographer by training. I also am an expert at retouching, developing, tinting, and the like. I just arrived from Salt Lake City two days ago, and I'm looking for work, so I thought I'd ask if you have anything or know of anyone who might."

The woman smiled. "My name is Freda Albrecht; I am a photographer as well. My husband, Wolfgang, and I own this studio. Please wait here, and I'll get Wolfgang."

Midori opened his coat and thrust his hands into his pants pockets. He fingered Thumbprint and smiled. A moment later, Freda emerged from the back of the shop walking next to a man a head taller than her. Wolfgang wore a navy suit with a striped red tie. His hair was slicked back with no part. His face seemed to shine as the lights from the shop window played upon his nose and mouth.

Midori thought about pulling his coat around him to hide the fact that he wasn't wearing a suit, but he thought better of it as Wolfgang bore down on him. Freda introduced Midori to Wolfgang, and the three spoke of photography for the next thirty minutes with only occasional interruptions from customers.

Just as Midori was beginning to wonder if the conversation would bear fruit, Wolfgang turned to Freda with a twinkle in his eye and said, "You know, Freda, besides the fact that Midori here seems to have some good skills, I can think of another reason to hire him."

"Oh," Freda replied as Midori held his breath and looked on. "What is that?"

"Well, *mein frau,*" Wolfgang continued, "our customers already wonder about our allegiance to America, think about how they will feel if we hire Midori! Maybe they will stop focusing their concerns on us and transfer them to Midori!"

CHAPTER THIRTY-ONE

New York City, New York

May 15, 1944

As he sat at the counter at Schrafft's drinking his morning coffee, Midori composed a letter to Hede and George, knowing full well that it would be Hede who would reply.

Dear Hede and George:

It is Spring in New York and everyone seems happy that Winter has passed. With the war effort seemingly going better the mood here in the big city seems positive.

I am still living at the Y, but with my new job, I will soon be able to move to my own apartment. That will be a very happy day! The job is going well and I am starting to actually take a few pictures again, though only in the studio. I have told my parole officer about the new job and he said it's okay.

How is everyone there? How are Papa Shimoda and Terazawa-san? And, the girls? And, of course, you two?

Please tell the Yamashitas I say hello. June, Susie, Sab, Asano. Teddy and Masakichi, too.

I miss and love you all,

Midori

Midori folded the letter and placed it in the stamped envelope he'd put in his pocket before leaving for work. He put the letter back in his pocket for mailing on his way to the studio. Having finished writing, Midori turned his attention to the New York Times as he continued to sip his coffee at the Schrafft's counter. The Allies were making significant gains across northern Italy, holding territory, and advancing. Midori had heard rumors that a major offensive would occur very soon, perhaps somewhere in France, though no one knew where or when. Or even if. Taking one last gulp, Midori folded the paper under his arm and headed out the door.

Although the Albrechts were wonderful people, they had a small shop and couldn't afford to pay Midori what he felt he was worth. Nor could they offer him any real advancement. So, after almost four months in their employ, Midori had applied for a position at the Robert Keene Studio on West 47th Street, just off of the famous 5th Avenue. The Keene Studio was much larger than Albrecht's, and there was a great deal of commercial work to be done.

Robert Keene was only too happy to hire Midori as his studio was overflowing with work. Keene explained that while a student at Yale, he'd had a Japanese roommate whom he'd gotten on with quite well. But, Keene warned, if any of the studio's customers complained about Midori being Japanese, he'd have to let Midori go. Midori acquiesced to Keene's plan and quickly demonstrated his value. In just one month, Midori was being assigned the lead role on major projects, though only in the studio, after explaining to Keene that the FBI would not allow him to use any portable camera equipment.

Midori began work on magazine illustrations, furniture, fashion, and food shoots. Keene appreciated both Midori's eye and his patience, sometimes watching his employee set up a shoot for hours, and carefully shooting sets of test images before getting ready for a final picture.

As Midori walked through the door on this spectacular Spring day, he noticed a lot of activity. Keene motioned to him, and Midori hustled over to his diminutive, wild-haired boss.

Keene smiled. "You know that I love that you are shorter than me, right, Midori?" he asked.

"Yes," Midori smiled, "you tell me every day! Looks like we are very busy today," Midori continued, motioning toward the group that seemed to be frenetically setting up a shoot.

"Food shoot. Just came up out of nowhere. Their other studio must've messed up because these folks contacted me very late yesterday in something of a tizzy. Anyway, it could be very lucrative. I'll need you to get involved."

Midori nodded but made no move toward the action. Keene smiled as he'd seen this reaction before. For the next thirty minutes, Midori stood ten to twelve feet from where the shoot was being set up and watched. Finally, he moved slowly toward the set. After introducing himself to the models, he approached a leggy young woman who towered over him and asked her to accomplish a quarter turn to the left. He placed the jar of mayonnaise that was the object of the shoot, on the table next to the model. Then, he placed her palm on the table next to the jar. This went on for hours until Midori finally began shooting on the set. By day's end, Keene and Midori had developed and re-touched the shots, and they were on their way to the client.

As he walked home, Midori pondered what he could have done differently. Lost in thought, he automatically made his way along the city streets until he reached the Y. He made mental notes of the changes he'd make next time. As the sun set, Midori entered the Y, carrying his dinner in a paper bag. "Next time," he thought. It wasn't so long ago that there didn't seem as though there'd ever be a next time.

HAPPY TO BE WORKING AT ROBERT KEENE STUDIO, C. 1945

CHAPTER THIRTY-TWO

New York City, New York

May 20, 1947

Three years and the whole world had changed. Not just for Midori, but, in fact, the entire world. The war was finally over and, while Europe and Japan struggled, America boomed. And, for once, Midori was not the odd man out. So many good things had happened that Midori sometimes just shook his head in wonder and smiled at his good fortune.

Baby Sano awoke every morning by 6:00 AM. Midori was more than happy to arise with Sano and to give him a bottle so June could stay in bed a bit longer. June would be with Sano all day, so Midori relished his alone time with the baby even if Sano constantly squirmed about.

As he fed Sano, Midori glanced at the wedding picture on the small table to his left. There was no doubt that June was a beautiful bride, but Midori thought to himself, "she's even more beautiful today than she was then." The war was still raging when June had left Salt Lake City to head to New York in September of 1944. At first, Midori thought of her as a family friend, but that soon changed, and thus began a whirlwind courtship. The two went to the opera, numerous Broadway musicals, and hotel clubs to listen to the big bands, including Guy Lombardo at the Roosevelt Hotel on New Year's Eve.

Midori laughed as he recalled walking by Bigelow's Pharmacy just before Christmas, only three or four months after June's arrival. He had stopped, walked into the store, and, almost on a whim, called June. At that moment, June happened to be talking to Vivian Reed, one of Midori's biggest professional fans, who had offered June a place to live at her recently purchased townhome.

Midori laughed even more as he remembered stating quite undramatically, 'You are going to marry me next year." As June later explained to Midori, she had told Vivian who, without a moment's hesitation, said 'Say 'yes!!'

Exactly one month later, they were married on January 14, 1945, at Vivian's townhome, which was also now June's home. The guest list included Vivian's family, a few of Midori's friends from Seattle, the crew from Robert Keene's studio, and the couple's friends from their favorite Japanese restaurant. And, June's mother, Asano, who had recently moved to Denver, had somehow scraped together the money to take the bus to be at the wedding.

Midori's smile broadened further still as he remembered the wedding day. Somehow, despite the privations brought on by the war, the day had been one of grand celebration. Food, wine, wedding cake, and flowers. And ribbons. Midori's buddy from back in Seattle, Kenji Nogaki, had done some work at Bloomingdale's and was able to borrow stations connected by ribbons to create a wedding aisle. Martin and Vivian Reed's brownstone on East 93rd Street became the place of lasting memories.

Sano finished his bottle so quickly that Midori did a double-take. The preemie was now a growing ten-month-old. Midori put his tiny son over his shoulder, and it didn't take much to coax a few burps from the little boy. Midori could hear June stirring, and he brought Sano to her. He kissed his wife and then headed off to shower and get ready for work.

Midori was sitting at the kitchen table drinking his morning coffee and reading the newspaper when there was a sudden insistent knocking on the door. He stood, briefly glanced at June, and Sano and headed for the door. He undid the latch and opened the door to see two men in suits holding badges.

"FBI, are you Midori Shimoda?"

"I am. May I help you?"

"We've got some questions to ask you, is there somewhere we can go so as not to bother your wife and baby?" the taller agent asked as he motioned to June and Sano.

"This is our whole apartment. I'm not sure what you have in mind, but we could go outside. There is a quiet park across the street, especially at this hour. Will this take long, as I have a very important photo shoot at work today?"

"Well, that all depends upon your answers, but, no, I don't think it will take long."

Midori kissed June and Sano goodbye, whispered, "don't worry," and asked the agents to give him a minute to grab a jacket. He walked into the bedroom, found his jacket, and then slipped Thumbprint into his pocket. He re-emerged and followed the agents out the door.

Midori and the two FBI agents found a wooden bench and sat down. They were awkwardly seated next to each other, and partially facing the sun, which caused Midori to squint. He turned slightly to the side and tried to focus.

"Okay, Mr. Shimoda, my name is John Tess, and my partner is Matt Johnson. Can you please tell us what you are doing for a living these days? You said you have an important photo shoot. Please explain that."

Midori clasped his hands together and held them on his lap as he answered question after question from the agents. They first asked about employment and then about Midori's personal life. Eventually, they got around to asking about his political beliefs.

Thirty minutes after their jarring intrusion, the FBI agents left Midori to continue with his day. He bounded up the steps back to the apartment and let June know he was okay before walking briskly out of the building toward the studio.

It was shortly after nine when Midori got to the studio. Robert Keene approached him and asked, "Is everything okay? It's late for you? Sano keep you awake?"

"I'm sorry, Robert," Midori responded, "it was not Sano. I had a friendly visit from the FBI."

"Seriously?" Keene replied.

"Seriously," Midori nodded.

Keene shook his head, then turned his attention to the left side of the studio. There, a beehive of activity was underway. Midori followed Keene and quickly jumped into the fray. As cameras were set and products placed at Midori's direction, Keene slipped away. Moments later, Midori spied him talking to his nephew, Jack, who worked at the studio. With them was a young woman of uncommon beauty. Her ivory skin was as pure as a newborn baby's. Her hair its own shade somewhere between brown and blonde. She wore bright red lipstick, and she walked with confidence beyond her youth.

Midori looked up as the trio approached. Keene smiled and said, "Midori, this is our lead model for today. She's just taken the train up from Philadelphia."

"Hello, Midori," the young woman said, "my name is Grace. Grace Kelly."

Midori took her hand and replied, "it's nice to meet you, Grace; I look forward to working with you."

GRACE KELLY FEATURED IN EYEGLASS PRINT ADVERTISEMENT,
C. 1947. PHOTO BY MIDORI

MIDORI AND JUNE MARRIED C. 1945

MIDORI AND JUNE C. 1945

JUNE, SANO, GRANDMA SHIMODA AND GEORGE WINTER
1946-1947

EPILOGUE

Midori Shimoda finally became a U.S. citizen on May 27, 1955. Before that, he was ineligible for naturalization due to the Immigration Acts of 1917 and 1924, which barred Asian immigrants from becoming citizens. From the end of the war in 1945 until he became a citizen, he was visited by the FBI, more or less annually, despite having never done anything even remotely to deserve such scrutiny.

Midori opened his studio overlooking Bryant Park in New York in 1949. After a long search for just the right setting for the studio, Midori found what he was looking for in a Beaux Arts building similar in style to the New York Public Library, Grand Central Station, and the Metropolitan Museum of Art. The building was designed and built for artists with spaces featuring tall windows and northern lights. And, the space Midori leased had a loft that would allow him to conduct two shoots at once.

As Midori was signing the lease, the real estate agent shared some history: The space had once been used as an apartment where William Randolph Hearst kept his famous mistress, Marion Davies. Needless to say, the irony of occupying the space once used for the "alternative life" of the leading antagonist of the Japanese was not lost on Midori.

Midori's work ethic and natural ability lead to his studio becoming a great success. He became a favorite food photographer for numerous advertising agencies. His still images were featured on brand labels for decades. Midori worked with many name stars in addition to those who tried modeling in the hope of breaking into theater or movies. His work included assignments with Grace Kelly, Betty Hutton, Gloria Swanson, Tyrone Power, Guy Williams, and Twiggy.

In addition to their eldest child, Sano, Midori and June had a second son, Dori, born in 1949 and a daughter, Risa, born in 1955. The couple raised their family in Dumont, New Jersey, just a bit more than a stone's throw from Midori's New York City studio. All three children have distinct memories of spending time at the studio on weekends.

Midori died on September 13, 1996, at the age of 85 after suffering from Alzheimer's Disease for nearly 20 years. Approximately six years after Midori's death, June was reunited with Midori's Blanding roommate, Devon Hurst. Devon shared with June that he had joined the armed forces immediately upon graduation from high school, much as he'd promised to do. He became a fighter pilot, was in the air and witnessed the bombing of Hiroshima, the birthplace of his former roommate, Midori. Devon also confided in June that he'd lived with a lifetime of guilt related to Midori's arrest after Devon had borrowed the Chevy Coupe. June assured Devon that Midori had never held him responsible for the arrest.

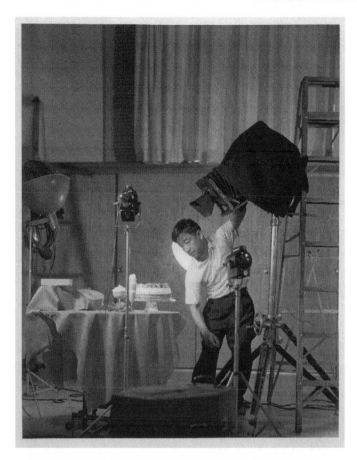

SETTING UP A SHOT AT MIDORI STUDIO, 80 W. 40TH ST. NY C.
1960

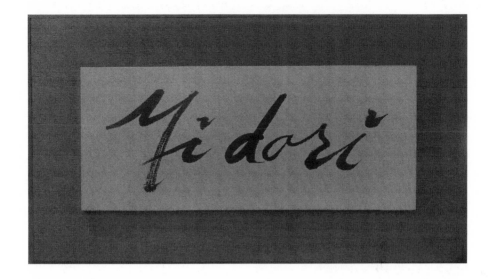

MIDORI INC. STUDIO SIGN

AUTHORS' NOTES

While growing up in northern New Jersey in the 1960s a grade
school classmate once asked me, upon hearing my mom was

born on a farm in Utah, "Where in Japan is THAT?" I shared that it is located "to the east of Nevada and north of Arizona." A half century later I am proud to know its mountaintops to valley floors are now in-demand destinations and treasured by visitors who come from around the globe to enjoy its spectacular desert vistas, limitless sky and opportunities to play outdoors.

The impetus to tell this story began with a road trip from Salt Lake City down to Southern Utah and up to Missoula, Montana to simply visit people and places that provided the backdrop for Dad's journey to the region during World War II. My mom, Aunt Susie, and I drove through vast landscapes and dramatic canyonlands in the wondrous state from which they hail, and where they met Midori.

Our first stop was Provo at a strip mall restaurant where we met Devon Hurst, Dad's one-time roommate, who was keeping himself busy in retirement as a Walmart greeter. It had been 57 years since Midori was arrested after his car—driven by Devon--was spotted out of town in the vicinity of nearby vanadium mines. The then seventeen-year-old Devon and his friends were walking the creek and hanging out in the welcome summer shade, never imagining they would return home to learn Midori had been taken to jail and the family's brownie cameras and arms confiscated.

Devon expressed sadness and guilt, feeling responsible for Dad's arrest and knowing he'd been unable to share this or offer an apology to Midori or his family--until that day.

From there, Mom, Susie and I visited other members of the Hurst Family in Blanding, some of whom remember Dad's short tenure in town or vague references to his having been around. Those who were kids remember him as the guy who had to learn the difference between the front and the back of a bridle to out-fit the family horse. They also remember Midori as the subject of casual arguments among neighbor kids about whether or not he was 'a spy.' He befriended enthusiastic photography buffs, including the Blanding High School principal, Ernest Biggs, who traded dark room time for producing and developing outstand-ingly handsome photographs, both for hire and volunteered, in-cluding one of the high school's 'Victory Queen' Audrey Adams in the 1942 *Piñon* yearbook. After meeting members of the Oscar Parley Hurst family and neighbors who remember him, his sister Setsuko, and niece May's presence in Monticello and Blanding that year, my family and I have come to appreciate the honest curiosity, generosity and acceptance expressed and ex-hibited by (almost) everyone in town.

From Blanding we headed to the north country and The Histor-ical Museum at Ft. Missoula, where elements of the Alien Deten-tion Center remain. We saw evidence of a possible renovation of the hearing room and museum. Interestingly, there were no books or historical materials discussing this period available in the gift shop. Asked about the availability of such materials, the shopkeeper simply commented, "That was a period of time about which we're ashamed, I'm afraid." Curious if the Museum archives included any evidence of Midori's detention, my sis-ter-in-law Karen combed through them during the next months and found stills of Midori preparing for a play of some sort, in costume. Interestingly, he had been asked to play a female, likely due to his being much younger than his fellow first gener-ation, Japan-born internees.

Sensing the lack of information about this unusual chapter in the annals of Ft. Missoula aside from seeing a handful of photos of Midori in drag, the evaporating remains of records of my dad's life in Blanding, and his subsequent ability to thrive and meet his life's goals despite the uninvited challenges, I sought assistance to assemble Midori Shimoda's story. Over a half dozen return visits, many emails and phone calls between 2002 and 2019 to Monticello, Blanding and Salt Lake City to meet with Devon and members of the Hurst, Lyman and Shumway families since 1999 have helped me get to know Oscar, Lynn Lyman and others who contributed to the fabric of the community. I have also met with the publisher (now retired) of *Blue Mountain Shadows* regional magazine, LaVerne Tate, and her family-based publishing team who suggested of other helpful resources.

Realizing the uniqueness of my dad's path as an 'all-American' kid <u>and</u> enemy alien simply trying to ply his trade while encountering fear and war-based detours and roadblocks, his story seemed too good to simply store in our family scrapbooks. Those who'd hosted and befriended him as a result of his 'voluntary evacuation' to Utah would not be around too much longer, so I made the effort to get to know them.

Others outside of Utah have been extremely helpful as well. The professional staff at the Historical Museum at Fort Missoula have since shared additional images of the Ft. Missoula Alien Detention Center and have connected us with producers of the documentary *An Alien Place* produced to tell the story of the Fort's role in this unsettling chapter of US history.

The second wonderful resource has been Densho, through which I was able to find a two-inch thick file of declassified documentation of my dad's incarceration, from his first arrest and the dozens of interview transcripts of his clients and neighbors, to his ultimate parole.

Of course, the best resource for the narrative is my mom, June, who decided to write down everything she could remember about Midori's story once she realized Dad, whose memory and countenance had suffered from a nearly twenty-year tussle with Alzheimer's, could no longer help tell his story.

My most vivid recollections of my dad are helping him pull weeds in the garden, watching and waiting for him at the lumber yard as he shopped for walnut or rosewood intended for a painstakingly crafted jewelry box, silverware chest or furniture for my bedroom; or holding glued component strips he let me hold in place, even though the wood clamps were plenty strong enough.

One predawn spring morning we sat in our back yard at a dew-laden spot for what seemed like forever to a five-year old, alongside a tripod-mounted Hasselblad camera. As we crouched in silence, he pointed out the pretty sky, the beautiful green of the arbor vitae and pachysandra nearby and the marvel of the tomatoes as they emerged from flowers in our garden. I wasn't sure what we were waiting for until a bumblebee visited and lit amidst the grass on flowering white clover: Dad took a number of shots until the bee departed. He folded up his gear and let me carry the tripod inside to join the family for breakfast and never mentioned what he'd been up to until he developed the contact sheets of the shots to choose one to enlarge and frame. Many weekend mornings were just like this as I watched him prepare, wait, and seize an opportunity to capture his appreciation of nature in print.

Dad endured a heart attack when I was seven. Soon after I graduated from high school, he both retired and started his twenty-year journey with Alzheimer's yet continued to apply meticulous attention to photographic subjects. He created stunning framed arrangements of autumn leaves and handsome lineups of smoothed rocks along walkways beside our home. Even in his last year at a nursing home in Denver, North Carolina he would thoughtfully place a salt and pepper shaker and recently received get-well cards along the window's ledge, then rearrange them again the next day, just so.

Midori talked about Blanding, but never about the narrative of this story. He shared his appreciation for the opportunity to learn how to make ice cream, bake bread and ride a horse with the Hurst family. He expressed a love for the desert before, during and after trips to wander and take pictures with his longtime friend Floyd Evans. He was not ignoring or hiding the absurdity of having to leave his business, stand silent to accusations of espionage, or face the dark side of being born in Japan unlike his siblings, who were born on US turf. He lived his truth in the moment, every day.

WHITE CLOVER AND BEE C. SPRING 1960

The pursuit of telling a story about a man born with enormous patience and an eye for creating real-life images became a journey to discover the generosity, empathy and alignment of kindred spirits. Many people played a role in preparing Midori to pursue his life's goal. They are an inspiration I hope will be shared by those who read these pages.

Collecting materials has taken time, but the reality of sharing Midori's story is due solely to the intellectual curiosity, smarts and invaluable friendship of my co-author, Bob Fleshner. While I cannot return the enormity of the online research, interviewing, drafting and iterating, I share his commitment to this project so that others may know his capacity to seek excellence for others to learn, love and share in his pursuit of his own truth.

Risa Shimoda

December 2019

Sometime in late 2018 my childhood friend, Risa Shimoda, casually mentioned that she had a proposal she'd like me to consider. Did I want to work with her on a "project?" Since I have an enormous reservoir of fondness for Risa, my inclination was to simply say "yes," and jump in. Little did I realize what Risa had in mind.

The Shimoda household was one of those central meeting places when we were growing up in small town New Jersey. Everyone was welcome and everyone was fed. Still, my recollection was that the main parental presence was always Risa's mom, June. I tested this theory with another childhood friend who had spent even more time at the Shimoda household than I had, and he agreed. Midori was polite and friendly, but somewhat remote, and always working on something or another. As it turns out, I was about to learn a whole lot more about Midori.

Once she knew I was committed, Risa handed me a box of documents. It was an eclectic collection ranging from copies of old magazine advertisements that Midori had photographed to official internment documents signed by none other than the infamous J. Edgar Hoover. The depth of research that Risa had undertaken was astonishing and made it easy to get to know Midori. Re-creating the timeline was another story, but, eventually, we brought it together.

To facilitate the narrative, we reconstructed many conversations since even those with nearly flawless memories can't be expected to remember verbatim discussions from 75 years ago. That being said, to make certain we got those situations right, we researched all of the facts that went into painting the individual scenes. For instance, for the trip from Pasadena to Utah, we examined the dates/times of FDR's fireside chats, the call letters of the local radio stations and the programming, the weather, and the range Midori's Coupe could attain (miles per gallon x size of the gas tank in gallons) on the trip.

We based the descriptions of Midori's many enemy alien hearings directly upon reports filed in the National Archives. Based on our investigations we are confident that we've captured the essence of these hearings both in terms of content and outcome.

A few characters are composites of a number of people. Most notably in this category are Robert Landers and Masao Nishi. We have extensive research that depicts the conditions in the Salt Lake City jail and in Fort Missoula. We also have significant information about wardens, sheriffs, and other similar members of the law enforcement community. But, our information on cellmates was less complete. We had letters from Midori while he was in Fort Missoula, and interviews with Susie and June, who visited him multiple times during his incarceration in Salt Lake City. From this information we were able to deduce Midori's frame of mind. We employed Robert Landers and Masao Nishi to further the narrative in a way that we believe fully captured Midori's nature.

Our goal in researching and writing this book was simple: to share with the world the story of a man who was extraordinary in the way that he went about his business no matter how high the odds were stacked against him. An extraordinary man, living in an extraordinary time, wanting nothing more than to live an ordinary life.

I am forever indebted to Risa for inviting me along on this journey. Her passion for the project was evident from the first moment. It was also highly contagious. Risa did all of the heavy lifting and then let me have the majority of the fun. It's hard to think of a better partner.

Bob Fleshner
December 2019

ACKNOWLEDGEMENTS

Over one hundred individuals have contributed to this work with advice, encouragement, facts and 'best as I can recall' recollections of my dad's path and passion. Near strangers have tracked down evidence to address a curious inquiry and a few folks have resolved long-held harbored or barely-shared sentiments and remembrances. Family members have contributed generously to connect personalities and places, and professionals whose expertise and professional responsibilities include tending to and organizing historical tapestries have responded to institutional requests with enthusiasm, interest, empathy and offers to assist further.

This project is possible due to the input and interest of family, friends and perfect strangers who either knew and loved my dad or who understand the importance of telling stories of the Japanese whose lives were permanently altered by fear of the unfamiliar. The most important character in Midori's story is his bride June, who years ago filled a spiral bound notebook full of recollections shared over the course of fifty years of marriage. She's since marveled at the trove of names, places and timestamps written to support endless elements of detail as my dad slid into a fog created by a lengthy voyage into the world of Alzheimer's-related dementia. She captured priceless stories and reflections without which we could not have attempted this project. She also provided crucial input as the manuscript evolved as its first reviewer and arbiter of whether the recounting of Midori's decisions and actions fit the footprint of the man whose life she shared. Many others read early drafts and provided insightful commentary including Jenna Litschewski, Jay

Weinstein, David Landau, Russ Fox, Carol Koenigsberg, Amanda Tarpey, Rachel Nathanson, Susan Debad, Christiaan Collins, and Bob's family members, Phyllis Aaronson, Michelle Fleshner, Daniel Fleshner and Irene Fleshner. Marijo Wright provided excellent copywriting and commentary as well.

In the daunting effort to seek a publishing partner, friends have offered help by reaching out to their own circles: Jeff Duncan, Kristen Regina, Pope Barrow, and Maria Isabel Hernandez-Frangenberg, Kelly Wheeler Bartlett, and Darcy Gaetcher.

College classmates Sammy Papert, Scott Dingwell, Ellen Petrill, and Lori Gibson Banducci helped brainstorm resource options for the project.

Our extended family members in Blanding and Monticello have been joys to meet. They have helped us understand why Dad appreciated the earnest but fragile support of Peter, Ada and DeVaughn Jones; empathic generosity demonstrated by Oscar Parley Hurst; non-traditional kinship of photography enthusiasts Ernest Biggs and Lynn Lyman; Parley Redd who allowed him to advertise his portrait-taking skills in the window of his Parley Redd Mercantile; and friendship of Maggie Harvey, Devon and Joan Hurst Mosley. We thank these folks many times over, and apologize for anyone we have missed: Etta Doreen Hurst, Nancy Hurst Dutcher, Dennis and Cathy Hurst Cosby, Scott Young, Clyde and Clark Harvey, Amy Isom, Bruce and Jess Cornwell, Charlotte, Steve and Karen Mosley, and Emma Myers, and Don Combs.

Blanding native and historian Gary Shumway introduced us and our inquisitiveness about Midori's stay in Blanding to many neighbors and friends. We thank Harold, Joe and Clisbee Lyman; Lynette Biggs Snow, Ruth Jones, and Steve Neilsen and Donna Neilsen Jensen for confirming our historical references and giving us permission to use family photos taken by Midori in 1942.

While the process by which Midori connected with his sponsor in Monticello is not completely clear, members of his host family have been gracious and open to our efforts to explore the circumstances related to his very brief stay. Thank you Fredric Hansen Jones, and Cooper and Colleen Jones for your input and suggestions.

A few dear friends are no longer able to join our celebration of Midori and his story. Nevertheless, we thank his lifelong friends whose mutual respect and love could have not run more deeply: Ken Huang Koda, Carter Winter, Vivian Schulte, Ed and Gloria Burnett, Nick Preston, and Gordon Hamilton.

Institutions

Each organization we contacted in search of a fact, timeline, name or photograph showed great interest in this project and extended themselves to support, corroborate and deepen our understanding of the events that surrounded Midori and set the stage for the events that unfolded before him. We thank them, their institutions and communities:

Aiko Yoshinaga Herzig, volunteer for Densho; Matt Lautzen-heiser, Carolyn Thompson, Ted Hughes, Kristjana Eyjolfsson, and Jessie Hughes at the Historical Museum at Fort Missoula; author Carole Van Valkenburg; documentary film producer Kim Hogberg; the dedicated and knowledgeable staff at the US Archives II in College Park, Maryland; the Japanese American National Museum and Dennis Reed; Lisa Crane, Pomona College Special Collections Librarian; Deborah Holmes-Wong, Director Digital Librayr and Metadata Team, and Stacy Willams, USC Libraries; Rhett Ariston, Whittier College Special Collections; Pasadena City College Shatford Library staff, Joy Painter, CalTech Library; Salt Lake City Archives; Daryl Tucker, Springville Area Historical Society; Lee Measom, volunteer, City of Springville, Utah; Mayor Toni Turk, Chris Webb, City of Blanding; authors James Aton, Bob McPherson; LaVerne Tate, Edge of the Cedars, San Juan County Historical Society, and *Blue Mountain Shadows*; Becky, Carrie and Jacob Joslin, *Blue Mountain Panorama*; Annette Tidwell, Farmington, Utah Historic Preservation Commission, and the knowledgeable online staff at turfonline.com.

Made in the USA
Coppell, TX
09 May 2020